# Stitching Stolen Lives

## AMPLIFYING VOICES, EMPOWERING YOUTH & BUILDING EMPATHY THROUGH QUILTS

### THE SOCIAL JUSTICE SEWING ACADEMY REMEMBRANCE PROJECT

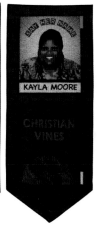

**Sara Trail and**

**Teresa Duryea Wong**

**C&T PUBLISHING**

Text, photography, and artwork copyright © 2021
by Social Justice Sewing Academy

PUBLISHER: Amy Barrett-Daffin

CREATIVE DIRECTOR: Gailen Runge

ACQUISITIONS EDITOR: Roxane Cerda

MANAGING/DEVELOPMENTAL EDITOR: Liz Aneloski

COVER/BOOK DESIGNER: April Mostek

PRODUCTION COORDINATOR: Zinnia Heinzmann

PRODUCTION EDITOR: Alice Mace Nakanishi

PHOTO ASSISTANT: Gabriel Martinez

FRONT COVER PHOTOGRAPHY:
• *Row 1 (L to R):* Anita Nowacka; SJSA; Kati Douglas *(hidden)*
• *Row 2 (L to R):* William Cooper *(hidden)*; SJSA *(hidden)*;
Amari Dixon *(hidden)*
• *Row 3 (L to R):* SJSA; SJSA; Kati Douglas; Teresa Duryea Wong
• *Row 4 (L to R):* Kati Douglas; Carter Gaskin

PHOTOGRAPHY by Social Justice Sewing Academy, unless otherwise
noted above or in Additional Photography Credits (page 174)

Published by C&T Publishing, Inc., P.O. Box 1456, Lafayette, CA 94549

Library of Congress Cataloging-in-Publication Data

Names: Trail, Sara, 1995- author. | Wong, Teresa Duryea, author.

Title: Stitching stolen lives : amplifying voices, empowering youth &
building empathy through quilts : the Social Justice Sewing Academy
Remembrance Project / Sara Trail and Teresa Duryea Wong.

Description: Lafayette, CA : C&T Publishing, [2021] | Includes index.

Identifiers: LCCN 2021019853 | ISBN 9781644031384 (hardcover) |
ISBN 9781644031391 (ebook)

Subjects: LCSH: Social Justice Sewing Academy Remembrance
Project. | Commemorative quilts--United States. | Textile crafts--
Social aspects--United States. | Murder victims--United States--
Portraits.

Classification: LCC NK9105 .T73 2021 | DDC 746.0973--dc23

LC record available at https://lccn.loc.gov/2021019853

Printed in the USA

10 9 8 7 6 5 4 3 2 1

When you take a step back and look at the sheer size of
the SJSA Remembrance Project exhibit, you will quickly
realize the tragic fact that the list of victims far exceeds the
capacity of a memorial project like this one.

## Acknowledgments

The Social Justice Sewing Academy is a grassroots organization. The very nature of *grass roots* means there are blades of grass spread in so many communities and in so many diverse populations that it would be impossible to acknowledge every name of every person who contributed to SJSA here on this page. We are incredibly grateful to thousands of volunteers, donors, students, workshop participants, facilitators, families, and sponsors, as well as all the makers who have stepped up to help us raise voices, remember the victims, and honor their lives. Your time, talent, and support are sincerely appreciated and treasured. We also appreciate those of you who have taken the time to read this book. It takes a village. The SJSA community is a powerful band of advocates and "artivists." We thank you for your contributions.

# CONTENTS

## by Reverend Jesse L. Jackson, Sr.

Merriam-Webster's dictionary tells us a metaphor is a figure of speech in which a word or phrase literally denotes one kind of object or idea as it is used in place of another to suggest a likeness or analogy between them.

In 1984, for my speech as a presidential candidate to the Democratic National Convention (DNC) in San Francisco, I was searching for a metaphor to modify and build on the idea that America is a *melting pot*. **A melting pot suggests that while there are many different ingredients that go into a pot, they are mixed together in such a way as to transform them into *just one* or *all the same*.**

In one sense the melting pot metaphor is correct for America. While we are different and come from many different places, that which binds us together *as one* is the Constitution. We also share a few ideas as well—for example, that each *individual* is important and a belief in *equal opportunity* for all.

In San Francisco I used two metaphors as I said, "Our flag is red, white, and blue, but our nation is a *rainbow*—red,

yellow, brown, black, and white—and we're all precious in God's sight. America is not like a blanket—one piece of unbroken cloth, the same color, the same texture, and the same size. **America is more like a *quilt*: many patches, many pieces, many colors, and many sizes, all woven and held together by a common thread.** The White, the Hispanic, the Black, the Arab, the Jew, the woman, the Native American, the small farmer, the businessperson, the environmentalist, the peace activist, the young, the old, the lesbian, the gay, and the disabled make up the American quilt. Even in our fractured state, all of us count and fit somewhere." The idea of a quilt is more representative of what America is than a melting pot.

*Stitching Stolen Lives* tells us of a worthy and working project. It reminds us of the unnecessary loss of life, especially young lives. It changes the lives of the workers and the beneficiaries of their work. It reminds us to love our neighbor as we love ourselves, and of the consequences of hate. It reminds us of the joy of weddings and the tragedy of unnecessary funerals. It keeps hope alive through remembrance of those we loved and of those whose lives have been stolen.

*Stitching Stolen Lives* takes the idea of the quilt to a different and even deeper psychological and spiritual level. It embraces the use of a real quilt for weddings, funerals, and remembrance of our loved ones. It reminds us of the importance of seeing and touching. It allows the quilt to bring back memories, exceed our feelings, and connect our souls. It amplifies voices past, empowers the quilters, builds empathy, educates, and activates for justice. It reminds and tells us there's power, healing, and remembrance power, in a quilt.

# FOREWORD

## by Hillary Rodham Clinton

Memories can bring comfort and courage. They can also bring grief and fury. How a person balances these competing emotions defines his or her character—and how a community responds to lives snatched by violence determines its future.

*Stitching Stolen Lives* calls us to feel so much: sadness, anger, love, determination. At the same time, it challenges us to reach for empathy and to forge the relationships that are crucial to strong, safe communities.

Each stitch in each quilt, in each of these banners, is a bold, brave stride toward that safer, more just world. Each piece reflects a life that was lost and the love that remains. **Each piece is also an invitation to speak out, organize, lobby, and use all our skills to make our neighborhoods and our nation places filled with joy and possibility rather than fear.**

These artists know this, and their art compels us to act.

The Social Justice Sewing Academy gives volunteers the space to do the essential work of creating and building community. **These artists, volunteers, and students give voice to their memories while working together to raise their voices—one stitch at a time—to create resistance, hope, and of course, art.**

I am grateful for their talent and their courage—for the healing they bring and the history they preserve. Because the Social Justice Sewing Academy quilters are historians as much as they are artists. They painstakingly record voices, transferring each syllable onto fabric. They show us the past in unflinching candor and help us see what must be done to heal.

Quilting has always been a powerful tool. In our nation's earliest days, women of all races—none of whom could vote—turned to quilting to preserve the past and illustrate their dreams for the future. Now, as people of all races all over our country work to combat gun violence, bigotry, and a pandemic, the Social Justice Sewing Academy teaches us once again the beauty and power of this art—and spotlights the essential role of young voices in building the world we need. That is just one reason why I am so proud that they agreed to create a quilt for the Clinton Presidential Center.

**We need these voices.** We need this art, full of strength and promise. And just as importantly, we need to heed the call to action woven into every stitch.

## In Our Own Words

**SARA TRAIL**

Founder of the Social Justice Sewing Academy

The murder of Trayvon Martin in 2016 devastated me. He was only fourteen days older than me. **Acknowledging the characteristics we shared forced me to consider the possibility that my life, as a young African American woman, could end in a similar way.**

At the time, I was making traditional quilts as a hobby and was a professional author of a quilting and sewing instruction book. I relied on numerous mentors in the quilting world to help me refine my craft, and while I enjoyed sewing in these quilting groups, I never once heard mention of Trayvon Martin's death in these spaces. The silence of the quilting community was deafening and alarming. The lack of response, or even acknowledgment, affected me deeply and shifted my perspective of how to engage with textile art. As a result, I founded the Social Justice Sewing Academy (SJSA) in 2017 to blend my love of sewing and quilting with my passion for advocating

against systemic racism, discrimination, and injustice. My first quilt in this new space was an appliqué art portrait quilt in honor of Trayvon Martin.

In the years since it was founded, SJSA has grown to be a nonprofit organization with thousands of volunteers in the United States, Canada, and around the world. Everyone who engages with the organization is a volunteer, as there is no paid staff; nor is there a headquarters building. Rather, this is a grassroots organization powered by the community. **We focus on a variety of programs, all of which are rooted in empowering individuals to see art as a form of activism and resistance.**

Our youth programs engage high school students and young adults in textile art to give them a platform to express their voices, frustrations, hopes, and individual challenges related to sociopolitical issues. When these young people finish their quilt blocks, the blocks are sent to a cast of hundreds of embroidery volunteers who hand stitch the fabric art pieces to a background. Once this step is completed, another set of volunteers combines these blocks into priceless community quilts. These community quilts have been widely exhibited around the United States and are a powerful tool to expose viewers to a different perspective. The goal of these quilts is not only to spark dialogue and encourage action, but to amplify the voices of the youth artists, whose thoughts and opinions are typically erased or ignored.

The SJSA Remembrance Project, which is featured in these pages, is a program wherein each adult volunteer is assigned the name of an individual who lived in his, her, or their community and who was murdered by police brutality, race-based violence, gender discrimination, or other violent means. Each SJSA volunteer is invited to memorialize a life that has been lost, through public information and reflection, prior to creating a quilt block that honors that individual. For some volunteers, this project helps to foster a deeper understanding of how systems within society—disproportionately and often negatively—affect marginalized communities. **The result of this newfound empathy and understanding is works of art, created by these talented volunteers, that for generations to come will help raise awareness of the ongoing efforts required to eliminate injustice.**

SJSA also frequently participates in other forms of community engagement, such as public lectures and interviews with magazines, newspapers, online media, and podcasts. It was during one of these interviews that I met Teresa Duryea Wong. We share a similar outlook, and we both are motivated to do what we can to raise awareness and encourage change. During our initial interactions, I realized the potential of Teresa's and my working together. We began communicating consistently, and before long, we agreed to collaborate to coauthor this book. Teresa created an original art quilt with a *Say Their Names* theme and has graciously donated it to SJSA.

**NOTE** *The authors are donating 100 percent of royalties from the sale of this book to the Social Justice Sewing Academy, a 501(c)(3) nonprofit organization.*

***REST IN POWER, TRAYVON*** 70˝ × 60˝ | COTTON | APPLIQUÉ | BY SARA TRAIL | 2017

**TERESA DURYEA WONG**

Author and lecturer

Getting to know Sara Trail has been one of the bright spots of my career as a quilt researcher, author, and lecturer. **I am so proud to be one of the many thousands of volunteers who are supporting the Social Justice Sewing Academy (SJSA).** I believe in this organization and its power to generate change. As SJSA continues to grow and gain traction, I feel that the organization will continue to thrive in this space as everyone involved works to raise awareness of the inequality and systemic racism in America, especially the inordinate amount of police brutality that happens every day.

Behind these stolen lives are husbands, wives, children, mothers, fathers, sisters, brothers, friends, teachers, neighbors, and families who loved them. Through the work of the SJSA Memory Quilts and Remembrance Project, we strive to remember how these individuals lived, not how they died. We want to share the stories of their everydayness, not their worst days. **We want to remember their dreams and the memories they left behind.** The days before their lives were stolen. And the days when they were loved.

SJSA is doing more than just saying their names. We are reaching out into the hearts and minds of countless volunteers. We are affecting those who view our quilts and textile art. And we are empowering youth to find their voices and share them. These activities will make a difference. We will not be ignored. We will remember, and we will make sure you remember too.

**SAY THEIR NAMES**
65″ ROUND | COTTON | APPLIQUÉ
BY TERESA DURYEA WONG | 2020

"The artivist (artist + activist) uses her artistic talents to fight and struggle against injustice and oppression—by any medium necessary. The artivist merges commitment to freedom and justice with the pen, the lens, the brush, the voice, the body, and the imagination. "The artivist knows … when you make an observation, you have an obligation."

M. K. ASANTE JR., AUTHOR OF *IT'S BIGGER THAN HIP HOP*

**For centuries, humans have turned to quilts for comfort, for warmth, for ceremony, for art, and to share their voices.** Quilts have the ability to tell a story and preserve that story for as long as the threads survive.

In 2020, the Social Justice Sewing Academy (SJSA) launched two grassroots remembrance projects that rely on quilts to tell a story and send a message. These quilts are both objects of healing and records of injustice. Their message is simple. Lives are being stolen every day, and this is not okay.

The SJSA Remembrance Project asks makers to create textile portraits or use photographs digitally printed on fabric in addition to using other imagery to create quilt blocks to honor individuals who have been murdered. These lives are stolen either by police shootings and brutality; racial or domestic violence; hate crimes; gender discrimination; disappearances and murders of Indigenous women; and community violence. These blocks are collected from volunteers and then quilted into banners and displayed in public. These banners are not meant to provide comfort or warmth. They are sharing and preserving a message, raising awareness, fighting injustice, and turning volunteers into artivists.

The SJSA Remembrance Project is part of a long lineage of community efforts to create quilts to express either outrage or patriotism or to raise awareness for or against a cause. Records from as early as the 1830s document that American Quaker women made quilts with anti-slavery messages to raise funds for the abolitionist movement. Quilts were made in support of the Civil War and against it. Quilts were made to fight prohibition laws in the 1920s and raise awareness of women's rights during the suffrage movement. In the late 1980s, the famous AIDS quilts were born. This movement was started by Cleve Jones, and he inspired thousands of people to create huge textile banners, three feet by six feet, honoring victims of the AIDS epidemic. The panels were stitched together and first displayed in the nation's capital in October of 1987.

Tens of thousands of quilters have joined a movement to make quilts honoring military veterans. And in the aftermath of 9/11, quiltmaking proved incredibly therapeutic for thousands of makers who turned to working with textiles as a way to grieve. In recent times, we've also seen environmental injustice quilts, antinuclear quilts, anti-war quilts, and tons of political quilts, especially during the Trump Administration, with quilters expressing views both for and against that administration's ideas.

> "The Social Justice Sewing Academy Remembrance Project is solidarity in the form of a memorial. Recognizing the collaborative, archival, and at times activist work of quilts over time, this project situates the Remembrance Project in a long lineage of textile artwork that tells community history."
> ▨ SUZANNE SCHMIDT, PHD, SJSA EDUCATION DIRECTOR

In the midst of all these efforts sits SJSA. This organization's mission is drastically different from those of other art or craft causes. **SJSA is designed to raise awareness of a topic most Americans are uncomfortable discussing: social justice and systemic racism.** The vast majority of victims of murder who are memorialized through the Remembrance Project are people of color. Data prove that people of color suffer inordinately more trauma at the hands of law enforcement than White people. And as these banners are exhibited in public, viewers will come face to face with portraits of people whose lives were stolen.

A second SJSA program, Memory Quilts, is designed to help those left behind to heal. When a life is stolen, a quilt can offer a tangible memento to help keep memories alive. A quilt can wrap a grieving mother, keep a grandmother warm, comfort a father, or provide a calm place for a child to lie. For this project, makers are creating large, usable quilts honoring the lives of murder victims. In many cases, loved ones share shirts and jeans the person wore, which are then cut up and pieced into the quilt. Other quilts are made with photographs printed on fabric. The finished quilts are donated to the families.

A Memory Quilt is both a memorial to the victim and a celebration of his, her, or their life.

Both the Memory Quilt project and the Remembrance Project have unique advantages. They are simultaneously raising consciousness of an important social injustice and turning volunteers into artivists.

The term *artivist* was born and elevated in communities of color. It differs from the idea of *craftism*, which connotes the work of people with resources, those who have time and money and choose craft as a medium to deliver a message. Artivists, on the other hand, are individuals who feel they have no choice. They deliberately pursue art as a way to push for change and to express their outrage.

The volunteers who sign up for SJSA remembrance projects are painfully aware of the issues, and through the art of sewing and making, they are becoming artivists. They are connecting with their communities and making a difference. **Whether through film, rap, street murals, or quilts, artivists are proactively part of a movement to stop the violence, stop the shootings, and stop the stealing of precious lives.**

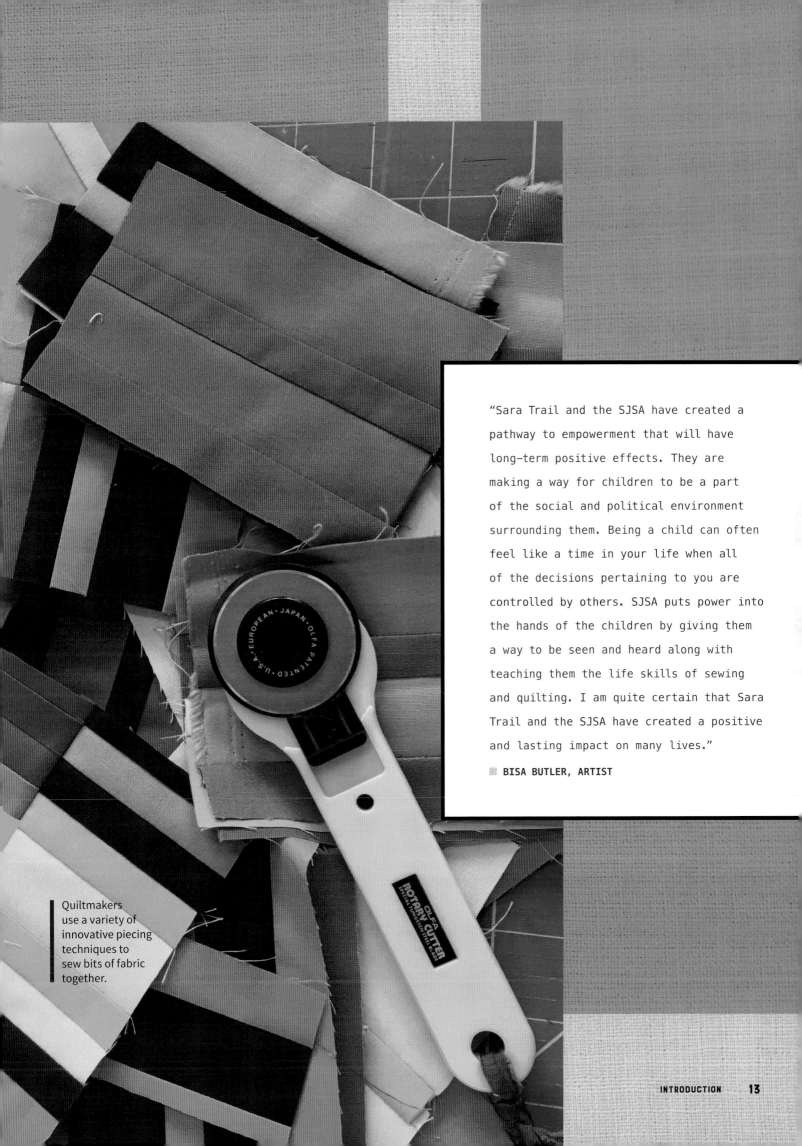

"Sara Trail and the SJSA have created a pathway to empowerment that will have long-term positive effects. They are making a way for children to be a part of the social and political environment surrounding them. Being a child can often feel like a time in your life when all of the decisions pertaining to you are controlled by others. SJSA puts power into the hands of the children by giving them a way to be seen and heard along with teaching them the life skills of sewing and quilting. I am quite certain that Sara Trail and the SJSA have created a positive and lasting impact on many lives."

BISA BUTLER, ARTIST

Quiltmakers use a variety of innovative piecing techniques to sew bits of fabric together.

JUNIOR
i'm a bird, you're a bird

Daniel

64

In memory of
Daniel Hernandez
Dodgers fan, Lakers man,

WORLD SERIES

14

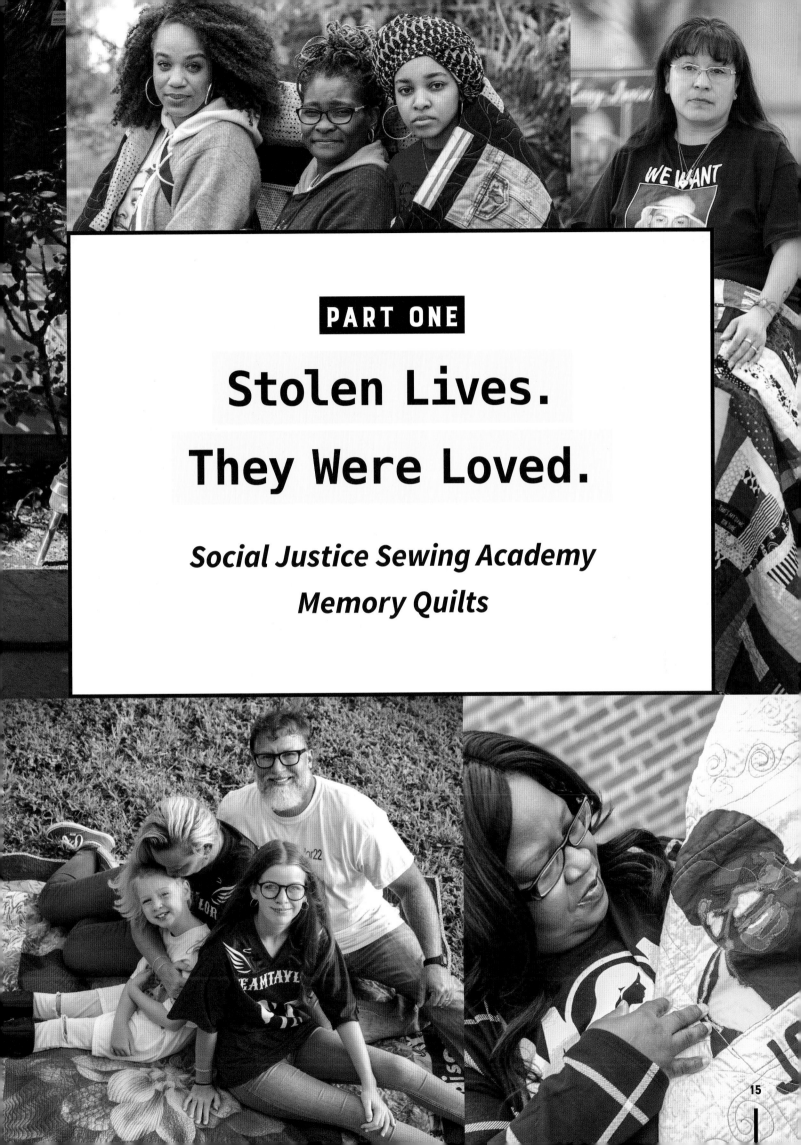

# PART ONE

# Stolen Lives.
# They Were Loved.

*Social Justice Sewing Academy*
*Memory Quilts*

# POWERFUL HEALING THE PROCESS OF SEWING A QUILT.

**POWERFUL HEALING THE PROCESS OF SEWING A QUILT.** The practice of cutting up cloth and piecing it back together, while strange to some, is wildly addictive for millions of men and women around the world.

For at least 200 years, sewists have turned to their craft to create quilts for ceremonial purposes, such as for births, weddings, and funerals. In the case of death, there is a long tradition of mourning quilts made from clothing worn by the deceased or quilts made in dark colors, such as black, that were traditionally used by families in mourning. In the nineteenth century, it was common to wrap men, women, and children in quilts for burial.

The Social Justice Sewing Academy (SJSA) Memory Quilts follow in the tradition of mourning quilts, but they differ in that these quilts are a celebration of life. They help families heal by bringing them into direct contact with their loved ones through the clothing stitched into the quilts. As pieces of a loved one's wardrobe touch our skin, we can feel memories. We remember how much we loved our lost one. And we are comforted when we touch the quilt.

If clothing is not an option, then the quiltmakers can rely on photographs printed on fabric. Other SJSA Memory Quilts are made with the person's favorite colors or imagery of things that he, she, or they cherished. These quilts bring people and their memories together. Families can literally wrap themselves in these Memory Quilts and find solace.

The SJSA Memory Quilts project extends awareness of a life that was stolen and gives families a powerful object that can comfort and heal. These quilts are visual reminders never to forget.

## The Stolen Life of Steven Taylor

*b. March 28, 1987 | d. April 18, 2020 (San Leandro, California)*

■ Steven Taylor was shot and killed inside a Walmart. The police officer shot Steven just 40 seconds after he entered the store. Statements from the investigation show that Steven was unarmed and made no threats to anyone in the store. Steven suffered from mental health issues, and instead of being given the help he needed, he was tased and shot, all in less than one minute.

**His family is fighting for justice.** They have formed an advocacy organization called Justice for Steven Taylor. At the top of that organization is one particularly powerful advocate. And she will not rest until there is justice. Meet Grandma Addie.

### Grandma Addie

Addie Kitchen is no ordinary woman. She spent 30 years working inside one of America's most notorious state prisons for men, San Quentin. And after raising a family of her own, she took in her daughter's three boys and raised them as well. One of those boys was Steven, who came to live with his grandmother when he was seven.

Tears were shed as Latifah Saafir presented the quilt made with Steven's clothing to his grandmother, Addie Kitchen.

Steven was a great kid. His teachers loved him, and his two brothers adored him. Once he reached school age, Steven was diagnosed with attention deficit and hyperactivity disorder (ADHD). As a result, he sometimes caused mischief and his teachers sent him to the principal's office for discipline. In middle school, during these incidents, Mr. Harris, a Black principal, allowed Steven to stay by his side throughout the day and follow him around rather than sending him home, calling his grandmother, or taking other disciplinary action. Mr. Harris believed in Steven and knew he was a good person, and he took the time to see this side of Steven.

Later in life, Steven wanted to be a barber. He loved cutting hair, and he cut hair for all his friends, even his beloved grandmother. **But mostly, Steven just loved being around people, and he loved music.** He loved to sing, and at one point he wanted to be a celebrity singer and entertainer. He spent countless hours inside a music studio at the home of a close friend. His grandmother thought that he'd make a good entertainer because Steven was outgoing and talented, and enjoyed being in front of people.

But somewhere along the line, all those dreams and ambitions went astray. As he matured, Steven struggled with his mental health and began to abuse drugs. It was difficult for Addie to watch. She did everything she could to help. She constantly talked to Steven, and all of his friends as well, about their life choices. In her words, she "raised hell" with those boys to get them headed on a better path.

When Steven reached his late 20s and early 30s, he chose to live in a homeless camp rather than live with Addie and abide by her rules. He returned to her home often to shower, do laundry, and eat a hot meal. Addie never knew when he would show up, but she always kept canned food and packaged goods at the ready to give to Steven to take with him. She gave him a mobile phone too, many times, but he never seemed to keep one for very long. The last time Addie saw Steven was in February 2020. Two months later his life was stolen.

In the immediate aftermath of the shooting, no official notified the next of kin of Steven's death. But word began to spread through the community, and Addie, Steven's mom, his brothers, and the mothers of his children received text messages from friends and heard rumors that Steven was involved in an incident. They all waited anxiously to find out what had happened and made many calls to police and hospitals to check on Steven.

Addie does not watch the recordings of those horrific events inside the Walmart. Yet as the news of this case has spread across the country, she has given many interviews to media and organizations. She will speak to anyone who is interested to learn about the injustice of this case.

As a former counselor inside San Quentin, Addie understands how the system works, and she knows what is broken. Steven's case is a classic example of what is broken, and there are many days when Addie struggles to understand why this happened to her Steven. **But one thing she refuses to do is to harbor hate and anger toward the officer who killed her grandson.** Rather, she is angry at the system that enabled him.

In an extraordinary expression of empathy, Addie feels that the officer was doing what he was trained to do, even though he clearly broke protocol. She believes that police officers today are not trained to deal with mental health problems. They are trained in weaponry and shooting skills, in the same way officers have been trained for the past half century. Addie recognizes that people have changed, times have changed, yet our officers are not trained in twenty-first–century tactics.

Addie Kitchen shared clothing worn by her grandson, Steven Taylor, with SJSA. When volunteer quilter Latifah Saafir received that box of clothing, she wanted to make use of every piece, so she constructed four quilts for the family. Pictured here is one of the quilts for one of Steven's sons.

T-shirts and jeans worn by Steven Taylor were lovingly incorporated into family quilts.

Justice for Addie means making big changes to the entire system. This country needs to reckon with its mental health crisis. There are no easy answers, but clearly, anyone who has ever tried to help a family member or friend through a mental health crisis knows firsthand how difficult it is to find professional help, and gaining access to long-term mental health treatment and recovery facilities is highly problematic for most Americans. Addie wants to change all that. For starters, she wants 911 hotline calls to be filtered to a variety of services, and professionally trained mental health staff and counselors should be the ones responding to 911 calls involving people in a mental health crisis, not armed police officers.

She recognizes that change is not immediate. In the meantime, she does not want the anger to consume her. She wants people to hear her voice. She wants them to understand that Steven had flaws, he struggled, he did not always do the right thing, but he did not deserve to die this way. Addie and others who knew and loved him are hurting. And they want justice.

## Advocacy: Justice for Steven Taylor

### Steven Taylor needed help, not violence.

As a result of his death, and the system that failed him, a dozen or so individuals have formed a nonprofit advocacy group to fight on Steven's behalf.

If you have ever wondered what exactly an advocacy organization named in honor of a deceased person does, well one action they have taken is to try to stop the repeated broadcasts of the recording of Steven's death. Steven's death and the recordings of it are not isolated incidents. In fact, these types of recordings are so prevalent they have their own genre, "trauma porn." In the year following Steven's death, every time there was an update on the investigation or trial, television news programs broadcast that same footage over and over. The Justice for Steven Taylor organization called several of those television newsrooms and asked them to stop. Some agreed and some did not.

These days, body cameras, smartphones, and security cameras have changed everything. We now have concrete evidence of events from these recordings. It's one thing for us, as viewers, to see this footage and have myriad reactions, including the option to ignore it. But imagine if you were Steven's family and you had to live through the trauma over and over. Or imagine if you were his friend, imagine if you were a mother, or a young Black man, or a young child, wondering if the same thing could happen to you. **Seeing this footage over and over keeps the trauma at the forefront. It cannot be ignored.** These scenes are a constant reminder that Steven's life was not valued by the officers charged with protecting their community. Hopefully, at some point, news media professionals will become aware of this trauma and broadcast these recordings only when absolutely necessary, in much the same way that broadcasters finally stopped broadcasting recordings of the planes crashing into buildings on 9/11.

In addition to the television advocacy, the organization pushes for action on a number of fronts. Through their website, they urge readers to make calls and take action. The site has an option to connect directly to elected officials in order to make your voice heard. The group has led protests and other activities to draw attention to the case and advocate against the tactics of the district attorney. Justice for Steven Taylor also acts as a watchdog and exposes political contributions and support from labor unions that are directed to elected officials and explains how these funds and political support are a roadblock to justice in cases like Steven's.

# The Quilter: Latifah Saafir

As one of the cofounders of the worldwide Modern Quilt Guild, Latifah Saafir is one of the famous quilters in a community of tens of millions of quilters. The quilters who know her name recognize and revere her talent for creating bold and beautifully quilted works of art. When Latifah teaches classes or presents lectures, her events sell out immediately. She is a superstar.

**But those who know her personally know that Latifah struggles with the lack of equality in the quilting world.** She is frustrated by the fact that within the sewing circles and quilt industry where she typically operates, there is no outrage over police shootings, no rallying cry to stop the violence, and no recognition of how these deaths disproportionately affect people of color. This is something she has always wanted to change, and the Social Justice Sewing Academy is one way to begin to change the world.

When Latifah saw a photograph shared on Instagram of SJSA founder Sara Trail with Addie Kitchen and clothing worn by Steven Taylor, she knew this was her opportunity. She reached out and asked to be given the opportunity to make his SJSA Memory Quilt.

As she began working on several quilts for his grandmother and sons, Latifah felt the full weight of her task. Clothing holds energy. And with Steven's clothing, Latifah knew these were the last things he wore. She was drawn to the texture of the denim jeans, and she found inspiration in the gold fabric of his shirts and sports jerseys. Traditional T-shirt quilts are very popular among quilters, especially for moms who want to preserve some of the dozens of T-shirts their children wear for events. The most popular way to showcase these is to create one large block for each shirt, then put borders on the block, add sashing and exterior borders, and then it's done. However, this was not the type of quilt Latifah wanted to create. In addition, she was very intentional about making quilts for Steven's sons that did not look juvenile, so they could have a meaningful keepsake as they grow older.

This clothing was special, and she wanted to make quilts that were special, too. She "talked" with Steven in her head, as she worked. She was incredibly thoughtful of every step of her process. Nothing was done without intense forethought. She made four quilts for his family. Each one has its own style, but they are part of a similar aesthetic. Steven's clothing is labeled so each family member can find it and recognize it and feel its energy.

Latifah's goal was to create a quilt that would comfort the family. She wanted to create little pieces of love. **There is no way to replace the life that was stolen, but these quilts of cotton and clothing will certainly help keep his memory alive.**

Latifah Saafir (*right*) shares a warm moment with Addie Kitchen.

## In Latifah's Words

"Today I get to open this box, I am scared. I'm overwhelmed. I'm honored. For so many years, the quilt world has stepped up and made quilts for the survivors of those killed in tragedies. Pulse Nightclub. The Vegas shooting. The shootings of police officers in Dallas. And countless more. Granted, there was a huge effort in the Charleston church shooting. Maybe I missed it, but I didn't see us step up when Trayvon Martin was killed. Nor for Eric Garner. Or Sandra Bland. Or Philando Castile.

Or… maybe I just missed it all. **So, when I saw the Social Justice Sewing Academy social media posts about Steven Taylor's story, and the subsequent post about meeting with his Grandmother Addie to accept his clothes to make a memory quilt, I asked to be blessed with the opportunity to make it.**

"I will open this box in private. But I plan on capturing my journey with this quilt. I feel like it's a huge weight and responsibility to get it right. I'm honored to be gifted this responsibility and will treat it with the dignity that it deserves. Somebody pass me a box of tissues and my rotary cutter. I've got work to do.

"The thing about my process is that the first part is internal and almost invisible. No pretty Instagram photos here. I throw all that I know about the person and the reasons I'm making the quilt into the back of my mind and I let my mind work through the details. At some point, the specifics of the quilt start to bubble up in my mind, and the puzzle pieces of the plan start to fit into place.

"The first thing I did was talk to Sara Trail from SJSA in detail about her conversation with Addie, Steven's grandmother who raised him. I wanted to know a bit about who he was as a person as well as a bit about his life story. I feel like we failed him as a society. In so many ways. Including but not at all limited to his murder by the San Leandro PD.

"It took me like two weeks to open the box of his clothes. I wanted to be alone and I wanted my mind to be clear and strong because I knew it would be emotional. And it was. The first thing I noticed was that the clothes all smelled like

fabric softener as if they were freshly laundered, and I just imagined Addie lovingly washing her grandson's clothing after his murder. Damn, where's my box of Kleenex.

"There were four T-shirts, one Shaquille O'Neal Lakers jersey and three pairs of jeans. I had already envisioned the quilt having denim in it, so I was excited to see the denim. The clothes were mostly dark with little pops of colors. I noticed all the T-shirts and the jersey shared that gold color that you see in a lot of sports teams, so I knew I would pull that out in my fabric pull. Part of what I learned in talking to SJSA was that Steven loved the Golden State Warriors and the color red. So immediately I knew I would have to incorporate both of these. I even bought a Golden State Warriors shirt to incorporate in the quilt.

"This whole quiltmaking process has been a long conversation between Steven and me. It is an act of deliberate love. I talk to him as I'm working. Having heard a bit about his journey from his grandmother Addie, I touch his clothes and wonder what they would say if they could talk as witnesses to his life experiences. I've made a conscious decision in my quiltmaking to put aside perfectionism. This project has not been about perfectionism but in every thought and every stitch in this quilt, I want to honor Steven in death with the care that this world did not give him in life. I'm very deliberate and very conscious of each decision. Everything is intentional.

"**Each quilt has a piece of each of the items of clothing that were sent to me.** Red is Steven's favorite color but I didn't want red quilts, so red is the pop of color in each of the quilts. Each quilt will also be backed in red. It is such a statement of power, life, and vibrancy, and yet it feels warm and comforting. I hope his boys and his grandmother feel the same. I wanted to be adventurous in the quilt designs, but with it being such an emotional process for me, I chose to go with existing designs. Addie's quilt is the most involved—it is the Put a Ring on It / Double Wedding Ring design using *huge* 18- and 24-inch templates so I could feature the T-shirts and jerseys that were sent. I chose the boys' quilts to both be simpler, so one is a Muffin Tops pattern and one is a Glam Clam. All the quilts look alike but each is very different and individual, which I love.

"It was such a bittersweet moment to finally finish these quilts. Today marks five months since Steven Taylor's murder. I can't wait to present these to his family. It feels like such a small gesture in light of their immense loss, but I hope it will bring some small measure of comfort."

As she worked through the creative process of making this quilt and incorporating his clothing, Latifah Saafir thought deeply about Steven Taylor, his life, and how the system failed him.

MAKER: ALI WALKER

### Steven Taylor Remembrance Block

"When I originally made this block, I wanted to focus on the injustice. It was shades of gray and red, and I wanted it to stand out. This was a man going through a known mental health crisis. This was a man shot because he held a baseball bat. This was a man with children.

"Our country deserves a better justice system. **Our people deserve to be seen for their intrinsic goodness, not their moment of sadness.** Steven Taylor was taken too early, and was not seen as a whole, wonderful, flawed human. This block is for Steven Taylor. Say his name."

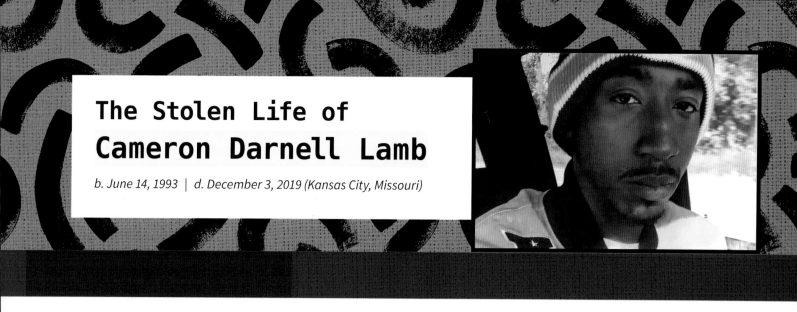

# The Stolen Life of
# Cameron Darnell Lamb

*b. June 14, 1993 | d. December 3, 2019 (Kansas City, Missouri)*

■ Cameron Darnell "CD" Lamb was born on June 14, 1993, to Laurie Bey and Bobbie Lewis Lamb. Cameron lived his life in Kansas City, always surrounded by cousins, friends, and family members of all ages. His life was filled with fun and many interests—music, sports, and cars. As he grew up, he was often described as "an old soul" because he loved old-school music and artists such as The Sugarhill Gang, Marvin Gaye, Clarence Carter, and the Isley Brothers.

**Cameron also was fascinated by Chevrolet automobiles and was called "Chevy Boy" by his friends and cousins.** Among his cousins and friends, he was probably the Kansas City Chiefs' most ardent and supportive fan, and he truly looked forward to the NFL playoff games and ultimately the Super Bowl.

He attended schools in the Kansas City, Missouri, school district, including Hogan Preparatory Academy, where he played football. He also played for the Ravens in the Pop Warner league. After high school, he worked at several warehouses until he found his passion—repairing cars. He realized that he had an entrepreneurial spirit and decided to couple his love for helping others with his passion for fixing cars.

Cameron had a tattoo ("God's Gift") on his hands, which became the inspiration for the name of his business, Cam's Gifted Hands. He used Facebook to grow his business, which became a mobile auto repair service. In addition to his mobile repair service, in the spring and summer months, he did lawn service with his cousins. **Cameron was "so excited" about the direction his life was taking.** He was filled with plans for a bright future—securing a home and furniture for his sons, growing his business, and spending time with his friends and his large, loving family.

When he was a young child, he accepted Christ as his savior and was baptized at his home church, Southside First Baptist Church, under the leadership of the Reverend Stanley Smith and the tutelage of his grandfather, Deacon Jason Pitre. At the church, he served in the choir and on the usher board.

CD had a priceless sense of humor even as a little boy. One day, when he was helping his grandpa mow the grass, he and his cousin kept trying to talk to their grandpa while the mower was on, but he could not hear them. However, when the two boys tried to devise a plan to get out of picking up trash by not mowing the grass in that section, their grandpa's sharp eye caught them immediately. CD came home that day and asked his mom, "How come old people can't hear, but they can see real' good?"

One day, while working his part-time mowing job, he finished mowing a neighbor's grass and knocked on the door to collect his money. Well, the homeowner took one look and realized he had only mowed half the grass. So she gave him half the money he was owed. Astounded, he asked her what was wrong. When she pointed out his mistake, he made sure never to make that same mistake again and learned a good lesson about wages.

**Cameron was a devoted father to his own children and a surrogate father to other children.** He constantly expressed his love of family and friends by always providing assistance, protection, and a life full of fun and laughter. In his parting words, "Love, peace, and soul, everybody."

**TOP LEFT:** Cameron Lamb's extended family in Kansas City, Missouri, is doing everything they can to keep Cameron's memory alive.

**BOTTOM LEFT:** Laurie Bey wraps herself in the warmth of this colorful, hand-stitched quilt made in memory of her son, Cameron Lamb.

**RIGHT:** Laurie Bey hugs the quilt honoring her son, Cameron Lamb, in Kansas City, Missouri.

**QUILTMAKER: JANE HILL STOKES**

## In the Words of Quiltmaker Jane Hill Stokes

"I was touched when I learned about Cameron Lamb. I have a son about his same age, and they were of similar build. I didn't know what to expect when I got Cameron's clothes, the information about his likes, and the photos from his family. I used the input from all those sources to help design the memory quilt. I added the yellow fabric for the Chevy logo and because the KC Chiefs colors are red and yellow, and some blues, because that was Cameron's favorite color, but otherwise I used the clothing fabric which the family sent. I chose the photos that I liked the best and incorporated as many photos as I could fit into the design.

**"As I started the quilt, I became totally focused on it, and after completing the piecing, I knew I couldn't give it to someone else to quilt.** I hand quilted it myself using a blue and black print for the back. The binding was done with gray fabric from a pair of the pants I was sent. I put my love into the quilt, and I hope Cameron's family can feel that."

## Cameron Darnell Lamb Remembrance Block

"Father, son, brother, cousin, and beloved friend. After looking at photos, watching videos, reading about Cameron, this block was created in his memory. There are hands (representing his) holding hearts with his boys' names, symbols for his love of Chevys and the Kansas City Chiefs, 26 solid stars (for each year of his life), and 53 unfilled and unfulfilled stars for the years that Cameron will not have (based on average life span of 79). **I kept Cameron and his mother, children, and loved ones in my heart while stitching, especially his mother's heartbreak of having her son become a memory.** I hope it holds the love he gave and that is felt for him."

MAKER: HAZEL C. MONTE

# The Stolen Life of Dominique Marcell Dunn

*b. May 28, 1992 | d. July 9, 2020 (Portland, Oregon)*

■ Dominique Dunn always hoped his mom would fix his plate for each meal. Even when he was a toddler, he would sit patiently and wait till she finished cooking and finally had a moment to hand him a prepared plate of food. And more than two decades later, at her 50th birthday party, his expectations were still the same. He hoped the mom he adored would fix him a plate of food.

On days when his mom would cook big meals for the whole family, with a smile on his face he would try to convince her to leave the whole pot of shrimp and grits just for him. She knew he was a "mama's boy," and that was just fine with her. **Ultimately, she would convince him to "pinky swear" that he would share her food with others. It was a game the two of them played often.** A son seeking all of his mother's attention. A mother's display of unending love for her son.

But his mom, Felicia Smith, also showed Dominique some tough love. When he was in high school his behavior changed, and he started getting into trouble. One day she dropped him off at the police station and left him there to think about the consequences of his actions. Another time, she signed him up as an ad hoc member of the Army National Guard. The sergeant in charge understood exactly what Felicia was trying to do, and he took responsibility for Dominique and put him through the same paces as actual reserve members. The exercises were grueling for a rebellious teenager and he was furious at his mother for making him go through all that.

But Felicia didn't give up. She kept taking him there for a full six-week tour of tough love.

Growing up, Dominique was close to his cousin Corey. For many years, the two were inseparable. Felicia's sister had six kids, including Corey. Their father had been a lifeguard, so all the cousins were strong swimmers, but Dominique was not. One summer Corey threw Dominique into the pool so he would learn how to swim the hard way. At first, Felicia was terrified, but that tough love approach worked, and Dominique learned to swim.

Dominique and his sister were also especially close, even though Dominique was four years older. He showed enormous pride when she advanced to high academic levels in junior high. And when her tutor came over to help with her homework assignments, Dominique always wanted to be there and "help" her by giving the answers. Felicia had to intervene and make him leave the room.

Years later, as his sister grew up and started her own family, Dominique was always welcomed as part of the family. His two nieces called him simply Uncle, not Uncle Dominique. He adored those girls and loved being their Uncle.

His love of children inspired his dream to one day work at a facility helping kids after school. He felt that this would be a great way to give back and help others in his community. He also loved music, especially rap, and was always writing his own songs. Music was a big thing in his extended family, and several of his relatives were accomplished jazz musicians. **Dominique dreamed of opening a music production studio of his own, where he could express himself creatively and also help foster the talent of young aspiring musicians.**

Ultimately, the mama's boy was always attentive to his mother. She was a big part of his world. Whenever she called his mobile phone, he always picked up, or if he was busy, he would call her right back. And, whenever the family was together, Dominique treasured her cooking and big love, especially when it was dished out just for him.

MAKER: MICHELLE FREEDMAN

## Dominique Marcell Dunn Remembrance Block

"Twenty-eight-year-old Dominique Dunn was killed by gun violence outside a club in Portland, Oregon, on July 9, 2020. Immediate reports shared misinformation, and rumors proliferated on social media. A rally was held while the family asked for privacy and a meeting with the DA. Dominique 'Domi' loved basketball and rap music. His smile was the kind that could light up a room. He was described as a family man.

"The star in this block is shattered points broken and floating away. The gold symbolizes his light and spirit. **A bright young man whose light was put out by a cruel and unnecessary act of violence.** May his family find the justice they deserve, and may they find peace in knowing that he is loved."

# The Stolen Life of Isaiah Lewis

*b. June 25, 2001 | d. April 29, 2019 (Edmond, Oklahoma)*

■ Love is one small comfort that Vicki Lewis clings to day after day. She knows deep in her heart that her son knew he was loved.

Isaiah Lewis thrived at his new school, Boulevard Academy in Edmond, Oklahoma. His teachers were friendly, and the classes were small. Thanks to the undivided attention from teachers and counselors at this alternative learning campus, Isaiah was able to get his education back on track and complete the five remaining credits he needed to graduate from high school. Along the way, he even earned awards for outstanding attitude and character. He was proud. And he wholeheartedly looked forward to his graduation day and being handed his high school diploma.

Like most teenagers, Isaiah had time management issues and somehow seemed to miss the bus every morning. Isaiah's parents were divorced, but the two families lived close together and he was co-parented by both his mother, Vicki, and his father, Troy. Vicki usually had the day off on Fridays and Isaiah always asked her to drive him to school. **Finally, one day when she was exasperated, she discovered that Isaiah had intentionally missed the bus because he thought his mom just liked driving him to school.** Looking back, she realizes the two shared a lot of love on those drives. Isaiah always hugged and kissed her goodbye and told her that he loved her. Those are extra moments that are now cherished.

Even when he was a toddler, he wanted to show his mom some love. One day, he decided he would help her cook dinner, and he somehow managed to drag a stool around the kitchen and fill a plastic bowl with water and beans.

Then, he set the bowl on the stove and turned on the heat. Fortunately, he quickly shared his achievements with his mother. When Vicki rushed to the kitchen, the plastic bowl was blazing.

He was the youngest of five boys—his two oldest stepbrothers are from his father's first marriage. Isaiah loved camping with his father and brothers, and he truly enjoyed traveling to their large family reunions in Georgia and Florida. All the brothers loved basketball, and Isaiah spent his early years being dragged from one basketball game to another. His brothers all lived for the game. Isaiah liked playing the game and his high school coaches remember him as a good player, but he was never as serious about basketball as his brothers.

**Music was his passion.**

He dreamed of working professionally in the music industry after graduation. He and his four brothers often rapped together in the family living room. And music is the thing that connected him to Amani Wallace, who quickly became a good friend at Boulevard Academy. Isaiah and Amani would meet up all the time, between classes, sometimes even during class, to share their latest songs. Amani always thought of Isaiah as a brother and the two grew close. She remembers how they would "boost each other up" over their musical creations. Each time they would part, they would say, "Let's go make another song."

It seems Isaiah's love of music developed at a young age. In third grade, he was selected by his teacher to learn to sing for a school program. **He never even mentioned this at home, but he loved learning the music and never seemed to have any stage fright.** Much to his mom's surprise, when the time for the performance came, Isaiah walked on the stage and sang his solo, as calm as ever.

Isaiah's first job was at McDonald's. He hated wearing the uniform and was not too thrilled with the work. So he hung on just long enough to earn enough money to buy a hot new video game, then he quit. As Isaiah grew, his mom saw him maturing into a young man. When a school event was coming up, he begged his mom to take him to buy a new suit. The photos of him wearing that suit are precious to Vicki now. **Behind the well-dressed young man in those photos, she remembers the real story of how he waited to ask her about the suit until the night before the event, like a typical teenager.** Isaiah called during her commute home from work and explained that he needed a new suit, then dropped the news that he needed it the next day! When Vicki got home, they rushed to a department store and were able to find a new red suit jacket, black slacks, dress shoes, shirt, and tie. Vicki was so hopeful when she saw her son all dressed up.

The night before he died, Isaiah lay on the bed with his mom and they talked for hours. They talked about so many things, but most poignantly they talked about racism and, as a young Black man, the need to be wary around police. She felt that Isaiah and his friends were just too young to truly understand the deep injustices caused by racism. She worried for them and she had "the talk" with Isaiah, and his friends, as often as she could. One of his very close friends, Lesha, heard that talk many times. She still visits with Vicki often, and they laugh and cry and keep his memory alive.

That night before he died, Isaiah and his mom eventually talked until they both fell asleep. Isaiah spent the entire night there on the bed next to his mom. But just before they closed their eyes, Isaiah heard his mom say, "I love you."

MAKER: HEATHER BRUMBELOW-SCOTT

## Isaiah Lewis Remembrance Block

"On May 18, 2019, Isaiah Lewis should have been wearing a graduation cap, not a halo. Isaiah was seventeen years old and murdered by police a month before graduating from high school. Isaiah was in the midst of a mental health crisis and running through neighbors' backyards begging for help. He was naked and clearly unarmed. Rather than de-escalate the situation, police tased the naked boy. When that didn't satisfy them, they shot him. There were no body cams. There were no eyewitnesses to the shooting.

**"While working on this project for the SJSA Remembrance Project, I kept coming back to Isaiah's mother's words.** Vicki Lewis shared, 'He doesn't get to graduate on May 18 like he could have. He didn't go to the prom. He didn't get his driver's license. There are a whole lot of firsts that he got to miss, and I don't get to see him for the rest of his life, for the rest of my life.' I approached this project with her feelings in mind. He should have graduated. He should have lived a long and beautiful life. Isaiah's portrait is based on his mother's favorite picture. I fashioned his name to resemble a high school letterman jacket. The final touch was the tassel. When photographed, no matter the angle or lighting, his halo refuses to do anything but *glow*. On May 18, he should have been wearing a graduation cap, not a halo."

# The Stolen Life of **Alex Flores Jr.**

*b. April 4, 1985* | *d. November 19, 2019 (Los Angeles, California)*

■ Alex Flores Jr. grew up in a working-class neighborhood in Los Angeles. When his large extended family got together for special events, Alex was always the one to get the conversation rolling. His father remembers that he was so talented at telling stories and seemed to converse with everyone so easily. It was one of Alex's gifts.

From a young age, Alex could see that his parents worked hard and struggled to realize their dreams. So he made it part of his mission to bring a smile to their face whenever he could. **Even though he was shy outside the home, he shined inside this loving home.**

Alex attended Jefferson High School, a largely Hispanic public school in LA. And even though he started out doing his best, he eventually made friends with a group of troubled young men and ended up quitting high school before he finished his senior year. At one point, Alex was incarcerated, and the family firmly believes that throughout all his struggles, he was ultimately let down by society. There were several incidents in which Alex was harassed, even brutalized, by police, and he had little or no recourse from these incidents. **He struggled to get good mental health care, which is an enormous problem so many Americans face.** After having served time in prison, and as a young Hispanic male with mental health illness, there were few job opportunities open to Alex. Like many young men of his age, he was failed by the system.

He and his sister Amanda were born just a year apart. For Amanda, it was difficult to watch Alex struggle in school and society. She knew deep inside he was a good person, and she could see his best side when she watched Alex spend time with her own children. Just like when they were growing up, Alex always managed to make his young nieces and nephews laugh.

Alex found his soulmate young and they were soon married. A decade later, his wife had persuaded Alex to enroll in a program to be certified as a dental assistant. They both saw this as an opportunity to stabilize their financial lives and provide excellent job opportunities. Alex was doing well in the program, and he only needed one more month to complete the certification when his life was cut short.

Alex's wife, parents, sister, and extended family will always remember his enthusiastic smile and his remarkable storytelling skills, and they take comfort in knowing that Alex shined in part because of his special place in this loving family.

## In the Words of Quiltmaker Karen Maple

"With the advent of social media, body cams, and 24-hour news programs, we are deluged with real-life footage, statements, and accounts of a staggering amount of cruelty in this world. **I sometimes feel overwhelmed, but I am also inspired to do what I can to help correct the injustice—or at least provide comfort.** I often make quilts that challenge people's world views and highlight injustices, and one of them was the senseless murder of Alex. The Los Angeles Police Department killed Alex in the bright morning light while he was holding a kitchen knife. Those circumstances simply felt incomprehensible. In making the quilt for Alex's family, I wanted to make something that truly reminded them of him and brought comfort.

"I started with no plan for the quilt. The family had noted that he loved the Raiders NFL football team and that the Virgen de Guadalupe was important to them. Finding the sports-themed fabric was difficult due to the pandemic. The Virgen de Guadalupe ended up dictating the design. I wanted her at the center of the quilt, figuratively radiating warmth to Alex. With the Virgin at the center, I decided to put Alex's heart next to her with the symbolic pocket from his black dress shirt. I included a few buttons. The rest of the quilt was a Log Cabin pattern made with his clothing, along with a strip of Raiders fabric. I hope the quilt brings back happy memories of Alex and continues to bring comfort to his family."

Alex Flores's mother is pictured in her home holding the lovingly quilted memory of her son. Quiltmaker is Karen Maple.

# The Stolen Life of Isaiah Rule

b. September 4, 2001 | d. May 5, 2020 (Visalia, California)

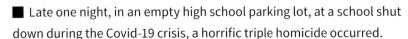

■ Late one night, in an empty high school parking lot, at a school shut down during the Covid-19 crisis, a horrific triple homicide occurred. Three teenage boys were shot while sitting inside their car. As of this writing, the case is still a complete mystery. **The mothers of these boys and their families are doing everything they can to keep this nightmare in front of the authorities and the public eye in the hopes that justice can be served.**

The families in this close-knit community within Visalia, California, have hosted candlelight vigils, balloon releases, and justice marches; once a month, they gather for barbecue picnics with friends of the three boys and their families to reminisce and keep their memories alive.

Nikkole Rule Balderama, mother of Isaiah, touches the SJSA Memory Quilt made for the family. Quiltmaker is Stephanie Baldwin.

Painted rock garden in honor of Isaiah Rule

Isaiah Rule's mother, Nikkole Rule Balderama, cannot begin to understand what happened that night. Isaiah was the oldest of four siblings and lived with his mom after she separated from his father while he was still quite young. As a toddler, Isaiah always wanted to be with his mom and cried when she left the house. When he got older, he was always serving as her protector. Even when they would be out running errands, if the car needed gasoline, Isaiah would be the one to jump out and pump the gas for his mom. He even wanted to protect his friends. Whenever he would drive a friend home, he would wait outside until they safely entered their home. **These small ways of looking out for others were an integral part of Isaiah's character.**

The eighteen-year-old always had a tight inner circle of friends, girls and boys, and their favorite place to hang out was at Isaiah's house. He was not involved in harmful behaviors that so many teenagers are drawn into. Rather, Isaiah was a good kid with a strong, smiling personality. He was the leader among his loyal group of friends and always the one they wanted to be with. Nikkole struggles to understand how this could have happened to her son, who had never even been in a fight with anyone and who did not have any enemies.

He attended a specialized charter high school, Crescent Valley II Public Charter School, in Visalia, and it was here that he flourished. This school offered Isaiah a chance to study independently and the one-on-one attention that he needed to keep his grades up and complete his credits. On the day he was murdered, Isaiah was just a few days away from his high school graduation.

While she makes every effort to keep her son's memory close to her hear, Nikkole Rule Balderama is also fighting for justice for his murder. Quiltmaker is Stephanie Baldwin.

Isaiah and his mom talked often about his future. Nikkole realizes that her son was more mature than most kids his age, perhaps because he was raised by a single mom and helped take care of his siblings, and thus learned responsibility at a young age. As he grew up, Isaiah was always thinking about what he could do for a career, and he and Nikkole talked about it a lot. Oftentimes, Isaiah steered their conversations to how he could take care of his mom in the future; specifically, he wanted to buy her a house and a new car. **Isaiah had already met with military recruiters, and he was seriously considering enlisting with the Navy, or possibly the Marines.**

Nikkole takes comfort in knowing that her son was a well-adjusted, loving, and mature young man. He was always smiling. And she learned later how much that smile meant to his friends and teachers; even teachers who knew Isaiah in elementary school remembered that smile. Certainly, as Nikkole and Isaiah's close friends Omar, Kevin, Dustin, Destiny, two girls named Mikayla, Hailey, Vanessa, Stephanie, Dom, Emanuel, Ryan, Jacob, Keke, Kenzie, and his girlfriend, Arlene, gather at those family barbecues, everyone is sure to recall that bright smile Isaiah always shared.

## In the Words of Quiltmaker Stephanie Baldwin

"Making a memory quilt honoring someone who has been lost to violence can be a uniquely emotional, but important, endeavor. In the case of Isaiah's quilt, I was given pictures of him as well as his favorite colors and music lyrics. I decided on an improvisational Log Cabin block design. Traditional Log Cabin blocks use a red or yellow central square to represent the welcome and comfort of the home, but since Isaiah's favorite sports team was the San Francisco 49ers, I used the scarlet and gold of their team colors as the center of each block. Light blue, lime green, and black-and-white blocks are embroidered with his favorite lyrics. **The finished quilt has a chaotic but joyful feel that I hope reflects a little of Isaiah's personality and brings his family some warmth and comfort.**"

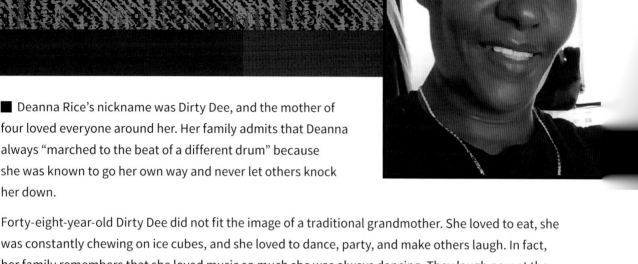

# The Stolen Life of Deanna Rice

*b. June 11, 1971 | d. June 8, 2020 (San Francisco, California)*

■ Deanna Rice's nickname was Dirty Dee, and the mother of four loved everyone around her. Her family admits that Deanna always "marched to the beat of a different drum" because she was known to go her own way and never let others knock her down.

Forty-eight-year-old Dirty Dee did not fit the image of a traditional grandmother. She loved to eat, she was constantly chewing on ice cubes, and she loved to dance, party, and make others laugh. In fact, her family remembers that she loved music so much she was always dancing. They laugh now at the fact that she was not a good dancer, but the thoughts and opinions of others never seemed to bother the boisterous Deanna. **She was her own woman. Yet, Deanna had a quiet side too. Even though she did not attend religious services, she often read her Bible for inspiration and for peace.**

When things got difficult, she still maintained her infectious laugh. And there were a lot of difficulties. Her own mother was forced to drop out of school in the sixth grade, later turned to crime to support her children, and eventually served time in prison. After a difficult childhood, Deanna raised her children in the impoverished Bayview–Hunters Point community on the edge of San Francisco. Starting in the 1940s, this region was home to a defense lab for the U.S. Navy, and it was widely known to be contaminated with toxic chemicals, yet this area was ultimately converted to low-income housing. Many residents suffered from the tainted water, lead poisoning, and other health issues. In addition, Hunters Point was riddled with crime.

Yet amidst all this, Deanna still managed to raise her children and keep her family together. In fact, she was happiest with the whole family celebrating birthdays or other events together. And her loving family was growing. Deanna was blessed with a new grandson just a short time before she was killed.

## In the Words of Quiltmaker Leonie Batkin

"Deanna's family sent seven photos of her life. She loved red, burgundy, gold, and music. Her seven photos reflected her beauty, grace, and life. After studying several design alternatives, I ultimately designed a Heart of Gold quilt. The piecing design in gold, surrounded by red, incorporates six of her photos, with the seventh image on the label. The quilting includes hearts, flowers, stars, and pearls to reflect her beautiful life. **What a humbling and honorable experience to grace Deanna's life with this quilt for her family.**"

Felicia Kenny, the daughter of Deanna Rice, and her family recall many precious memories while they lovingly touch the quilt made in honor of Deanna's life. Quiltmaker is Leonie Batkin.

IN MEMORY OF
DEANNA RICE

SJSA 2020

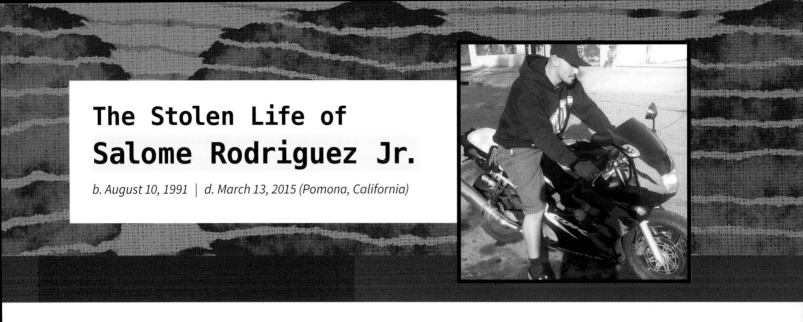

# The Stolen Life of
# Salome Rodriguez Jr.

*b. August 10, 1991* | *d. March 13, 2015 (Pomona, California)*

■ Salome Rodriguez, whom everyone called Junior, and his mother, Lidia, were inseparable. When they weren't working or in school, they spent a lot of their free time together, or they just sat and talked. When Junior was just ten years old, he learned to dance and loved dancing with his mom. Junior was also very protective of his mom, as well as his dad and five sisters and brothers.

**His mentor was in fact his own father, and Junior admired his hard-working attitude and the way he treated Lidia with respect and care.**

Junior grew up in a religious family, and at the tender age of eighteen he became a missionary. He found the work of spreading the message of his church very rewarding, and he often told his mom how joyful it was for him when he connected with people who were open to his message. He spent some time in Martha's Vineyard living with a local family while serving as a missionary, and he fell in love with this part of the country. He hoped to return there one day. He also fully intended to continue serving his church in one way or another throughout his life.

He loved horses and learned to ride when he was just two years old. Growing up, he spent summers at his grandfather's farm in Zacatecas, Mexico, and he rode his grandfather's horses every day. When Junior was twelve years old, the family spent the summer in Mexico.

He loved riding horses, but outside of that activity he was bored because all the other kids in Zacatecas were still attending classes, and he waited for the school day to end to be with them. The family asked the teacher if Junior would be allowed to attend classes there too, and several days later the family was informed he could attend this local school. This is where Junior first began to learn the history of this region of Mexico, and he was proud of the place where his father had grown up.

**A year before he was killed, Junior started getting tattoos to commemorate things that were meaningful to him, and he had the word "Zacatecas" tattooed on the back of his shoulder.**

Even though his father was not fond of the tattoos, Junior continued adding this art to his body. He even had an image of his mother and father tattooed, showing just how much he loved his family. Another arm tattoo showcased an image of Jesus and Mary.

He also loved riding motorcycles, and just a few days before his death, he had finished paying off the loan he acquired to buy his own motorcycle. The motorcycle fit his style because Junior loved to dress like a "greaser" or a cowboy in his favorite pair of Levi's, with a cowboy hat and boots. According to his friends, family, and girlfriends, Junior was a handsome young man.

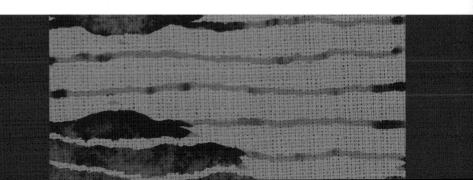

In addition to the motorcycle, he also owned a car and paid all his own bills, even at the young age of 23, plus he helped his family pay half of their rent. Just like his father, Junior was a hard worker, always. He spent so much time working, starting as a young teenager, that he didn't have much free time for friends, but he was close with three of his cousins.

Junior chose not to go to college. Instead, he was hoping to start his own business. **He was considering starting a moving company because he loved the idea of driving across the country and seeing life and nature in other states.** Every time he left the house, though, he made an effort to kiss his mom goodbye and tell her that he loved her. But even though travel was interesting, what Junior loved most was being at home with his close-knit family.

Salome Rodriguez, whom everyone called Junior, was brutally murdered in 2015 by a police officer, who later tried to flee. The officer was charged, convicted, and sentenced to 40 years to life in prison. Junior's brother and sister admire the quilt made to honor their beloved brother. Quiltmaker is Liat Rorer.

## In the Words of Quiltmaker Liat Rorer

"Working on this quilt has been one of the most meaningful and moving projects I've ever done. Years ago, I lost a brother to violence, and I watched what it did to my mother, so I had some understanding of how it feels to lose someone suddenly, in the prime of life.

**Every design decision I made was informed by the information I got from the family or from my research.** Salome was called Junior, the headline on the quilt. His favorite color was blue, so that is the predominant color, broken by white and yellow to represent the light and love of his family. He is at the center of the quilt and is surrounded by his family, Above him are images based on his tattoos and a saying he liked: 'If I'm a bird, you're a bird.' The quilting includes hearts, again representing love surrounding Salome, and was done prior to adding the photographs so as not to sew over them. The bottom of the quilt is faith-based, including a cross with 'Salome Rodriguez' embroidered on it. Most importantly, the quilt was made with love."

Lidia Rodriguez struggles every day to understand was brutally murdered and why his life, which was beginning, was stolen. She runs her hand over the quilt made in his honor. Quiltmaker is Liat Rorer.

# The Stolen Life of Daniel Hernandez

*d. April 22, 2020 (Los Angeles, California)*

■ Daniel Hernandez was incredibly proud of his fourteen-year-old daughter, and he looked forward to planning her quinceañera. When she was growing up, the two shared a special bond. They loved making homemade popcorn and watching movies together while talking and laughing. She was his whole life. On his way to dropping her off at school in the mornings, he'd sometimes stop to buy her snacks. And when he picked her up, he always checked with her to see if she was hungry or needed anything.

He was also especially close to his mother, and as Daniel got older, he did everything in his power to protect her. When she was sick, he was there to take care of her, even if that meant missing work. They would spend a lot of time together, and he tried to help her with her chores. When they'd do laundry together, Daniel loved to tease her to make her laugh. He would hold up his small nephew's clothes and ask, "Is this yours?" Another funny memory his mom recalls is when he'd take her and his daughter to the beauty salon. When he dropped them off, he'd jokingly say, "You both are ugly," and when he picked them up, he'd say, "Wow, you are both so beautiful!"

**Joking around seemed natural to Daniel, and he was always the one who laughed the most.** As a kid, he was the same way, always finding ways to laugh. One day he brought a live snake to his elementary school class, which he thought was hysterically funny. The teacher did not agree, and Daniel was suspended for several days. When the family was together, he would tease his young nephews by pretending to steal their food. Daniel spent many fun hours with his nephews playing video games, taking them places, and ordering lots of pizzas while watching movies and

television. Family members lovingly nicknamed him *el frijol*, or "the bean."

Besides pizza, one of Daniel's favorite foods was chile relleno, a Mexican dish, and he relished every moment when his mom cooked it for him. She also remembers how he loved her pancakes with fresh strawberries. Daniel's large extended family would often get together and share meals and special events. But Daniel always tried to avoid the limelight on his birthday, telling his mom not to bother making a cake when they could just go out to eat.

Family and friends recall how Daniel was quite reserved, even though he liked making others laugh. He didn't really talk that much. **He preferred to do things to show his love for family. For example, he once remodeled his mom's bathroom, and proudly told her a little bit of kindness goes a long way.**

Daniel had a lot of goals for his life. **He was a warm and friendly person; even his neighbors loved being around him.** Daniel also loved dogs and was working toward opening his own daycare facility for dogs. Now those neighbors, and his beautiful family, are trying to seek justice for his murder. It's a tough road for everyone, but his mother believes that one day they will all be together again.

**TOP:** The family of Daniel Hernandez holds a memory quilt honoring Daniel's life. Quiltmaker is Ann O'Callaghan Shoup.

## In the Words of Quiltmaker Ann O'Callaghan Shoup

"As I was cutting into the shirts given to me by Daniel's family, I wondered if he last wore them to work, to family gatherings, or was wearing one of them the last time he hugged his mother or his daughter. **I felt grateful to be making a quilt his family could wrap themselves in and be embraced by Daniel's memories.** I knew he was a big Lakers and Dodgers fan, so I added some of those logos and included Daniel's name in the Dodgers font. I thought he would have liked that. I hope this quilt brings some small happiness to his family."

# The Stolen Life of
# Taylor McAllister

*b. July 21, 1994* | *d. December 22, 2016 (St. Petersburg, Florida)*

■ Taylor McAllister was just 22 years old when she was brutally murdered in 2016 in St. Petersburg, Florida—a murder that has never been solved. She was the mother of young twin daughters, and the girls are now being raised by Taylor's parents, Bill and Leslie.

## Taylor adored her twin daughters and loved being a mom.

She was interested in cosmetology and spent countless hours with her daughters, and her two sisters, doing their hair and makeup. Taylor had a lot of dreams for her future—dreams that were never realized. Taylor's two sisters vividly remember how Taylor always kept them entertained watching movies late at night, laughing together, and hugging each other tightly during scary scenes.

Shortly before she was killed, Taylor taught herself how to play the guitar and enjoyed making music. When she was young, Taylor often belted out songs by the Spice Girls, and when she was older, she often sang as she played the guitar. Some of her favorite musical groups were The Cure and Justin Timberlake, and her family says her voice was truly angelic.

Bill and Leslie McAllister, and their family, sit on the memory quilt made in honor of their daughter Taylor. The family lives in Tarpon Springs, Florida. Quiltmaker is Teresa Duryea Wong.

Taylor is remembered as a loving person. **Her parents asked for her memory quilt to incorporate Taylor's love of dolphins, a natural affection for a young girl who spent most of her childhood in Florida.** The quilt also includes her favorite color, purple. Bill and Leslie work desperately to keep Taylor's memory alive and to search for justice for her senseless murder.

# The Stolen Life of
# Charles Raymon Glass Jr.

*b. November 19, 1970 | d. May 22, 2020 (Los Angeles, California)*

■ Charles Raymon Glass Jr. was a friendly man who knew almost everyone in his neighborhood of Los Angeles. Many neighbors called him by his nickname, Wizard. Charles liked to chat, and he joyfully shared his wisdom and advice to help his friends and neighbors.

**His favorite pastime was to stay home and hang out in the garage enjoying life and music.**

While his elderly mother, De'Lois Glass, was in the hospital fighting Covid-19, Charles was shot while walking along his street, just two doors away from his home. As of this writing, the case is still a mystery. But, for De'Lois, his daughter Kaylin, and the rest of his family, his passing is a tragic and senseless loss of a man they dearly loved. He was a son, a father, and a grandfather, and he will be missed.

De'Lois Glass and her granddaughter Kaylin E. Glass, Charles's daughter, treasure the quilt made in his honor. Quiltmaker is Stef Kingery (Jack and Theo's Quilting Co.).

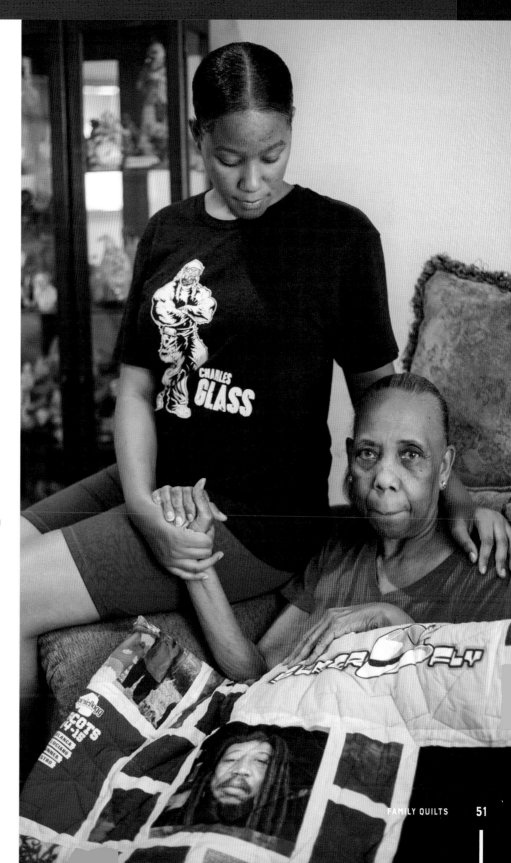

Mother and grand-daughter hold hands over the quilt honoring Charles Raymon Glass Jr. Quiltmaker is Stef Kingery (Jack and Theo's Quilting Co.).

## In the Words of Quiltmaker Stef Kingery

"There was an immediate energy surrounding the box of Mr. Glass's clothes. It was a reverence that came along for this entire ride. Before even attempting to review the articles of clothing, time was spent researching Mr. Glass's life and the legacy that was left behind. I felt like I had the chance to consult Mr. Glass on numerous decisions and collaborate with him to create this for his family. He loved his football Raiders and dogs, and his favorite colors were sky blue, dark blue, and money green. His favorite dusty brown Polo Ralph Lauren sweater was included in the box of items from his family and then found its way into his memory quilt.

**"To me, Mr. Glass resembled a great character actor out of a movie, and that served as my inspiration for his 'film strip'–style quilt.** My hope was to give him the starring role in the legacy quilt being created. His life mattered, his legacy matters, and I wanted his memory quilt to reflect those sentiments. But it was also important to me that his memory quilt be a joyful celebration of the unique human that Mr. Charles Raymon Glass Jr. was and that his family could draw both support and beautiful memories from it."

**LEFT:** The mother and daughter of Charles Raymon Glass Jr. show off the large, colorful quilt made in honor of his life. The quilt features several images printed on fabric, his blue jeans and Dickies pants, and icons from his favorite sports teams. Quiltmaker is Stef Kingery (Jack and Theo's Quilting Co.).

# The Stolen Life of Jesse Sarey

*b. July 10, 1992  |  d. May 31, 2019 (Auburn, Washington)*

■ As a young child, Jesse Sarey was extremely close to his brothers and over a dozen cousins. It was hard not to be close to each other when the children all lived in the same house and slept next to each other throughout their grandparents' home. His brother Torell described the area of Seattle, Washington, where they grew up as a neglected neighborhood, but their family bonds were strong and they all relied on each other.

Eventually, Jesse and two of his brothers were placed in a group home. Torell lived with Elaine Simons for nine years, until he aged out of the foster care system. Jesse eventually lived with Elaine, too, for about six months,

while he was in elementary school. One of Elaine's most memorable events with the boys was the day she took them to see a professional wrestling match. At first, as a woman, she dreaded having to go alone with the young boys to a venue filled with wrestling enthusiasts, but it turned out to be quite fun. She bought the boys costume wrestling belts and masks, which she thought were quite ugly, but the boys cherished them. Everyone had a great time! Jesse's brother remembers the day vividly and says they were truly "hyped up" at the time.

As a young adult, Jesse reconnected with Elaine and came to stay with her for several weeks. Elaine now

**BOTTOM LEFT AND TOP RIGHT:**
Kari Sarey is pictured here with Jesse's brothers (her three sons), Koleton Hart, Matthew Sarey, and Torell Sarey.

treasures that time because she was able to have that special memory. Elaine, Torell, Jesse's cousins Steven and Kelli, along with Steven's parents, traveled to Cambodia together during the time that Torell lived in Elaine's home.

Cami Vo, Debbie Pullen, and Janine Chu worked as supplemental literacy tutors at the school Jesse attended. Each of them cared deeply for the Sarey family. Cami was just eighteen years old when she began working in the program, and Jesse was in first grade. She has vivid memories of teaching him and considers him one of her special students. They studied together every school day for a half hour. Sometimes Jesse and his cousins would come to visit her before school started. **She remembers he was always quiet and well-behaved, and she always saw Jesse accompanied by one of his brothers or cousins. The family of kids traveled as a unit.** When Cami reconnected with Jesse years later on Facebook, he still talked about his family and told her he was still taking care of the "fambam" (his nickname for his extended family).

As a kid, Jesse loved sports, especially kickball and tetherball. **And like a lot of little boys, he was always jumping around, being active, and making funny poses to make his friends laugh.** As he got older, he took to basketball and it became his favorite sport. His brothers remember the time Jesse was able to participate in a special one-on-one youth sports workshop with Rashard Lewis, a basketball star with the Seattle Supersonics at the time. When he wasn't playing basketball as a teenager, Jesse was break dancing. He was known for his awesome backflips and spins. Just before he died, Jesse learned to snowboard. While he didn't have the time to improve, he enjoyed snowboarding immensely and discovered how much he truly enjoyed being outdoors.

The "fambam" now has to deal with a lot of emptiness without Jesse. Some days it is simply hard to cope. Jesse was a free spirit, and he took life in stride. Now that he's gone, the family hopes he will rest in power, and they plan to stick together to keep his memory alive.

*Special thanks to Torell Sarey, Matthew Sarey, Kenysha Sarey, Maryna Ream, Mary Sing, Elaine Simons, and Cami Vo for talking with SJSA over Zoom about Jesse and his life.*

Jesse Sarey's mother, Kari Sarey, holds tight to her son's memory and the quilt honoring his life. Quiltmakers are Tuna Chatterjee, Georgette Gagne, Gwen Marceline, Liz Marmion, and Lija Yang.

## In the Words of Quiltmakers Tuna Chatterjee, Georgette Gagne, Gwen Marceline, Liz Marmion, and Lija Yang

"For us, choosing to make a memory quilt for SJSA felt essential and also heavy with desire for change and justice. We were sent a photo of a beautiful collage that had been created to represent Jesse's life, and as we explored the different facets of the collage for inspiration, we were acutely aware of wanting to honor his life for his loved ones. The collage became our muse for the quilt. We spent hours studying it as we searched for fabrics and worked on a design that would capture a glimpse of Jesse's life and history.

"**We chose to make a double-sided quilt, one that represented the complexity of who Jesse was, that acknowledged his everyday life, his loves, and his struggles.** On one side, the lotus flower represents the ideas of peace, rest, and ultimately hope. On the other, we pieced his name in large letters to act as a banner for all the other blocks representing important parts of the life he lived. With the quilt label, we celebrate Jesse, the boy and the man.

"We experienced a mixture of emotions while sewing—sorrow, outrage, and humble reverence. Sorrow and outrage that his life was cut short by systemic racism, and reverence for who Jesse was in the world. As we worked, we grieved this young man and his family who live with this loss, and wanted to offer a place of peace and rest in the here and now, as well as hope for a better future. Mostly, we wanted to honor this young man by making a quilt that he might actually have gotten from a friend or family member."

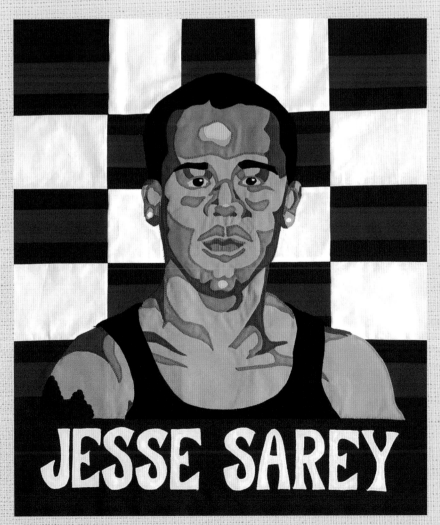

MAKER: LEEANNA BUTCHER

## Jesse Sarey SJSA Remembrance Block

"To honor the memory of Jesse Sarey (who was killed by an Auburn, Washington, police officer in 2019), I wanted to include his heritage as a Cambodian American, so I designed the background quilt block in the blue and red colors of the Cambodian flag. **I was also struck with the soulful expression in his eyes in the photos I found of him, and I tried to recreate that with my portrait.**"

# The Stolen Life of Anthony Nuñez

*b. January 6, 1998* | *d. July 4, 2016 (San Jose, California)*

■ Anthony Nuñez was a tall, skinny kid who loved to make everyone laugh. Laughter seemed to help ease the memories of his early childhood, which had more than a fair share of tragedy. His mother died just a few days after he was born, and he was raised by his grandparents until he was five because his father was unable to provide a stable environment for Anthony. Then, when Anthony was just five years of age, his grandfather died and later his grandmother also passed away, leaving Anthony with a second set of lost parents.

Fortunately, Anthony's biological aunt, Sandy Sanchez, and her husband, Jesse, adopted him and provided him a warm and loving family and a healthy environment while living in El Paso, Texas, for ten years, and later in California. Anthony was close to his older brother and considered him his mentor. **When he made the honor roll in elementary school, he told his mom how proud he was to be just like his big brother.** He also had a sister, and the two of them were very close in age.

As a child, his goofball antics showed up early. He was always dancing, joking around, and getting into mischief. One day in elementary school, when the students were painting with their hands, Anthony plopped his wet, painted hands on his teacher's backside, which he thought was pretty funny. Another teacher, who met Anthony when he was seventeen, as part of a program to teach art in the East San Jose high schools, remembers how Anthony's eyes lit up when he discovered they'd be creating poster art in class. **He was always quick to help the teacher by carrying supplies, and as usual, everyone in class knew they could count on him to liven up the atmosphere with a joke or two.**

Jesse and Sandy recall that there are lots of videos of Anthony dancing when he was young, and as he got older, he learned to rap and started writing his own music. His parents had just purchased a new speaker system for Anthony right before he was killed, and he installed the system in the garage, so his friends could come over and hang out with him there. When he was inside the house, he'd take whatever situation was in front of him and turn it into a rap song. For example, if his "mom" was in the kitchen cooking, Anthony would break out in rap to sing how his mom was the best mom ever. Maybe he did this to encourage her and make her laugh and stay in the kitchen, because he truly loved to eat.

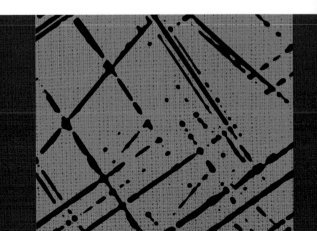

Sandy Sanchez adopted her nephew, Anthony Nuñez, when he was five years old. She recalls how he was a kid who loved to laugh. She misses him dearly and struggles to come to terms with his murder. Here she is wrapped warmly in a quilt made in honor of Anthony. Quiltmaker is Susan Compton-Smith.

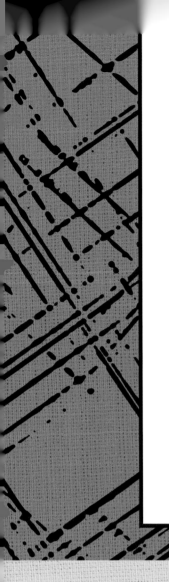

In high school Anthony made the football team, and he just loved playing football. His mom smiles as she remembers that Anthony also loved being around girls! His lifetime dream was to join the Army. **He often told his mom he wanted to serve in the military because he wanted to be a hero.** He once asked her to imagine a scenario where she is in the kitchen cooking and Anthony comes home, with his duffle bag tossed over his shoulder, and he rings the doorbell. It was a scene straight out of a movie, but sadly for Anthony, that dream was never realized.

He was killed late one night outside his family's home by two police officers, when he was just eighteen years old. Sandy cannot comprehend why officers showed up at her home with guns and tactical gear in response to a plea for help. As Jesse says, Anthony was really robbed of so much from day one.

Family and friends have launched a nonprofit organization to keep the memory of Anthony Nuñez alive and seek justice. The organization also advocates for meaningful changes in law enforcement and the judicial system.

## In the Words of Quiltmaker Susan Compton—Smith

"I signed up for the Social Justice Sewing Academy Memory Quilts project knowing that it would be an emotionally heavy quilt to make, knowing that I wouldn't know exactly how heavy until I began and that it would probably be heavier than I expected. Anthony was so young, just eighteen, when he was killed; he had not yet even had the opportunity to graduate from high school. When I received his name and basic information, I had to sit with it for a few days before I even began planning his quilt. I researched his case, learned about his family, his life, the things he had looked forward to in his future. **He was treasured beyond words by his family, and it is a solemn duty to create a quilt for a family grieving such an unfathomable loss.** Once I had had a chance to process my initial feelings of sorrow at his loss and anger at the broken system that caused it, I focused all my thoughts on creating the most beautiful tribute I could.

"When I received the box of his clothing to be used in his quilt, I could tell which were his favorite shirts by the amount of wear, and I made those the focal point of the quilt. I tried to imagine which combinations of clothing he would have worn regularly, which outfits would have been his favorites, and created the layout based on that idea. I wanted his family to feel Anthony when they looked at the quilt. I have long since completed Anthony's quilt. But I think of Anthony every day still, and I always will. There is a small piece of my heart dedicated to him."

Jesse and Sandy Sanchez. Quiltmaker is Susan Compton-Smith.

# The Stolen Life of Jocques Clemmons

*b. March 30, 1985* | *d. February 10, 2017 (Nashville, Tennessee)*

When Jocques Clemmons graduated from high school, he sent one of his senior portrait photographs to his favorite teacher, Mrs. Bowen. His note to her shared his most personal thoughts, and he thanked her for helping him "make it." Mrs. Bowen was White and Jocques was African American, and the two of them became close friends over the years. Jocques always used to tease his mother by telling her, "I've got two mommas, one is White and the other is Black."

Jocques's mother, Sheila Clemmons Lee, and his step-father, Mark Lee, raised him and his three sisters. Sheila worked hard over the years to provide for them. **But she could always count on Jocques to help her and support his sisters.** In fact, she remembers that he was always especially protective of his sisters and often took on the role of family leader. But his mature nature doesn't mean he didn't sometimes still act like a typical teenager. Sheila clearly remembers all the times he would wrestle his sisters to the ground and terrorize them the way brothers often do. His grandmother was worried when he'd wrestle with the girls, but his sisters seemed to take it in stride and laughed about it.

**It was Jocques's sweet smile and fun-loving attitude that kept the whole family laughing.** Even when his mother was tired or had a bad day at work, as soon as she would see Jocques, he would make her smile and laugh. He just had that way about him.

Sheila Clemmons Lee looks at the back of the innovative quilt made in honor of her son. Quiltmaker is Jenny Meakins.

As a young boy, Jocques dreamed of playing professional football and wanted to join the Dallas Cowboys. He, his friends, and his two cousins were always playing football. Jocques and his two closest cousins were all born about one month apart, and they seemed more like siblings than cousins. As they grew up, the boys loved being together and watching NFL games on television. **Jocques was also really good at working with his hands, and his mother says he was always taking things apart and putting them back together.**

Eventually, Jocques became a father to two children, and he adored being a father. His children's mother also had six other children, and Jocques became a biological father to two and a father to six others. He was so proud of all his children, and being with his family was the thing he loved most. And when his three sisters had children of their own, being an uncle was something Jocques truly cherished.

The large extended family struggles with his death and the aftermath, but deep down they all know that Jocques was loved, and more importantly, each and every one of them knows without a doubt that he loved and cared for them more than anything.

Sheila Clemmons Lee hugs the beautiful quilt made in honor of her son, Jocques Clemmons. Sheila lives in Nashville, Tennessee, the same city where Jocques was shot and killed by an officer with the Metro Nashville Police in 2017. Quiltmaker is Jenny Meakins.

## In the Words of Quiltmaker Jenny Meakins

"I will always remember the emotions I felt when I opened the box of Jocques's clothes and smelled the distinct aroma of fabric softener his mother had used before sending them to me. It took some time, and more than a few tries, to develop the final design for his SJSA memory quilt. From the many incredible photos and stories of Jocques, the details of the quilt emerged and centered on his love for the Dallas Cowboys while also representing his mother's experiences advocating for justice in his memory.

"In the end, I designed a two-sided pieced quilt with the colors and a star in honor of his beloved Cowboys while incorporating as many pieces of his clothing as I could. **I was told he was always smiling, and I hoped to capture that joy in an appliquéd portrait taken from a photo.** Finally, I added one last detail from a story I discovered during my research into Jocques and his mother, a pair of butterflies. The experience of making this quilt while learning of Jocques's life and loss is one I will never forget, and I can only hope that it brings his mother joy, warmth, and comfort."

Sheila Clemmons Lee and Mark Lee proudly display the beautiful quilt made in memory of Jocques. Quiltmaker is Jenny Meakins.

# The Stolen Life of Zarrie Allen

*b. November 23, 2001  |  d. July 20, 2020 (Sacramento, California)*

■ Anthony Charles Allen fought hard to make his neighborhood a better place. Like fathers everywhere, he wanted a community that was free from drugs and crime, and a safe place for his six children to grow up. His dream was especially difficult given that his community was known as the Iron Triangle neighborhood in the city of Richmond, California. The Iron Triangle, so named because of three railroad tracks that border the area, is the heart of Richmond's African American community. It is considered a high-crime area and a forgotten neighborhood.

Zarrie Allen grew up in the Iron Triangle. As a teenager, she lived directly across the street from the park that her father is credited with revitalizing. Anthony passed away in 2014, six years before Zarrie became an innocent victim of a drive-by shooting in Sacramento, a senseless crime and the very thing he feared most.

**Everyone who knew Zarrie remembers her brilliant smile.** She was a typical teenager who loved junk food and McDonald's. Cake was one of her favorite treats. But it was her grandmother's gumbo that was one of her favorite meals.

She was a track star, and some of her proudest moments came when she set new records in the long jump. She ran track at her high school, Salesian College Preparatory. When she was still quite young, she joined a community league, the Oakland Police Athletic League, and rose up through the ranks to become one of the league's most accomplished track athletes and to compete on a national level.

But track wasn't her only interest. Zarrie was curious about so many things. She considered a career in law, where she would stand up for the rights of people of color. She considered a writing career and often wrote poetry, short stories, and even rap lyrics, which she shared with her dad, who was an avid rap fan. **Ultimately, though, during her first year of college at Sacramento State University, Zarrie zeroed in on nursing.** She felt this was the career that fit her best and allowed her to do what she loved most, help others.

When Zarrie left the Iron Triangle to head to college, her sister Toniesha Bostic and brother-in-law gladly helped her pack up and drove her to "Sac" State. On the way, they let Zarrie choose the music to listen to while driving. Of course, Zarrie chose music that most teenagers love, and Toniesha, who is sixteen years older, was not fond of her music choices, but she let Zarrie be in charge since this was such an important day for her. Once they arrived, Toniesha helped Zarrie get situated in her new surroundings and decorate her dorm room.

Toniesha knew Zarrie would make new friends easily. Zarrie was always joyful, always smiling, and friendly to everyone. People were drawn to Zarrie, and so many of her friends, teachers, and mentors, even from her elementary school, remember that smile. One young friend recalled how she was often a loner at school and didn't have many friends. One day Zarrie walked right up to her and asked her if she had a friend. When the answer was no, Zarrie immediately replied, "I will be your friend." That moment changed the young woman's life. And for Zarrie, there were so many more moments like that one. **She touched so many lives in the same way, with friendship, kindness, joy, and lots of big smiles for everyone.**

**BELOW:** Zarrie's sisters, Attalah Allen (*left*) and Toniesha Bostic (*right*), and her mother, Anissa Jones-Allen (*center*), hold the quilt made in Zarrie's memory. Her blue jean jacket and other clothing were lovingly incorporated into this beautiful quilt. Quiltmaker is Erin Duane.

## In the Words of Quiltmaker Erin Duane

"When I learned about Zarrie Allen and her family's loss, I sat with her clothing for a long time, picturing this beautiful young woman wearing these track pants to her team practices and meets, throwing this denim jacket on over this comfy T-shirt as she headed out the door, cozying up on the couch with her loved ones in these sweatpants to watch a movie. As a mother myself, I spent a long time thinking about the loss Zarrie's mother has to battle every day … how that would make me feel and what I would want from a memorial quilt, to serve as a keepsake of my child. I knew once I landed on a design that reflected Zarrie's youth, energy, kindness, intelligence, talents, and beauty, I would be able to cut into her clothing to begin, but it did take me a very long time to settle on a design that felt 'right.'

**"After many sketches and revisions, I decided on a bold and simple design that really lets Zarrie's life speak for itself in the blocks.** I used her favorite colors (red and black) and incorporated African wax print fabric (she loved West African dance). I created a block with a book theme (she loved reading and writing), and I added blocks to honor her intentions to become a nurse and to reflect her strong religious faith. Working with the denim of the jacket was a creative way to include pockets that her hands had entered; I cut the jacket so that the pockets could be incorporated, allowing someone to share a pocket space with Zarrie. The large double **Z** in the center of the quilt is for the nicknames that her family gave her ('Zee Zee' or 'Z') … something about the nicknames really hit my heart hard, and I knew they needed to be a central element in the design. There's something so intimate about cutting into another person's clothes, in an attempt to reinterpret who they were, in an object for their loved ones. Zarrie is someone I wish I could have known, and creating this quilt (and a pillow with the remnants) for her family made me feel like I was part of her story somehow. She had so much more to give to the world, but I know that the time she spent here brought her friends and family light, love, and beauty."

**MAKER: ERIN DUANE**

## Zarrie Allen Remembrance Block

"Zarrie Allen was a few months shy of her nineteenth birthday when she was shot and killed while attending a memorial at a cemetery. Her killer has yet to be apprehended, so the incredible loss of her light and presence is topped with a lack of justice for her murder. Zarrie's future was bright, like her gorgeous smile. She enjoyed a variety of hobbies and interests including reading, writing, fashion, West African dance, and hair design. In creating this remembrance block for Zarrie, I struggled to decide which aspect of her story I would center on for the design. I ended up using a photograph, digitally printed onto fabric, because this photo speaks a thousand words. **Her kindness, her innocence, and her youth all emanate from this photo.** I then added African wax print fabric for her love of West African dance and a border of poetic typography to represent her love of reading and writing. The roses were a final touch to represent her inner and outer beauty."

# The Stolen Life of
# Stephon Clark

*b. August 10, 1995* | *d. March 18, 2018 (Sacramento, California)*

■ Stephon Clark was shot by police in the backyard of his grandmother's home. He was unarmed and holding a smartphone.

On the day that Stephon Clark's life was stolen, Se'Quette Clark says, the world lost someone truly special. **As a child growing up, Stephon was a gifted student who excelled in his school's engineering and science programs.** Outside of school, though, his mother says, he was a joyful and loving kid who loved to dance and was known to sneak up behind her and plant wet, sloppy kisses on her cheek.

Each year, as another anniversary of his deaths arrives, his mother and other family members, as well as his two children and their mother, struggle to cope with the loss of a young man whom they described as a man who had turned a corner in life. He was always a very caring person, and although he had his struggles, Stephon wanted most of all to be a good father to his two young children.

Stephon's brother, Stevante Clark, has become an activist fighting for change on behalf of his brother and all others who are unjustly killed by police and law enforcement. **Because of Stevante and the advocacy of other family members, as well as widespread protests and outreach by the community, after Stephon's death the city of Sacramento enacted a new policy that prohibits police from disabling body cameras and microphones.** In addition, the city also changed its policy on how officers pursue suspects. The names of the officers who fired the shots that killed Stephon were withheld for more than one year after the shooting, and no charges have been filed against the officers. However, Se'Quette believes that justice comes in many different facets. For her, knowing that the police officers involved in the high-profile deaths of George Floyd and Breonna Taylor face legal consequences is a form of justice for Stephon.

Se'Quette Clark and her daughter are wrapped in the love of the quilt made in honor of Stephon's life. Quiltmaker is Stef Kingery (Jack and Theo's Quilting Co.).

Stephon's mother, Se'Quette Clark, holds this timeless tribute to his life. Quiltmaker is Stef Kingery (Jack and Theo's Quilting Co.).

## In the Words of Quiltmaker Stef Kingery

"The first photo I saw that the family provided had 'Stephon's Life Mattered' written across the bottom. That phrase became my guidepost throughout the process of creating and bringing this memory quilt to life. His complex life and devastating death were both tough to reconcile with the handsome young man that I had looking back at me. The losses this family has seen are more than anyone should ever have to bear.

"I used Stephon's machine-embroidered initials, S.A.C., as the centerpiece for his memory quilt. His favorite nickname was 'Zoe,' an homage to his middle name, Alonzo. That name was hand embroidered in silver thread, featured just beneath his initials. **The intersections of the quilt blocks felt very much like the twists and turns that Stephon's young life had taken, running into an end here and creating a new beginning there.** I also created fabric letters from an oxford plaid button-up shirt. Wide flannel fabric created the warm backing that makes the quilt extra lovely to snuggle up with. A handwritten quilt tag was created for the back, with the quilt's motto and Stephon's birthdate and death date. My hope for this quilt and his family receiving it, is that it brings a small level of comfort and fond memories of a life cut way too short."

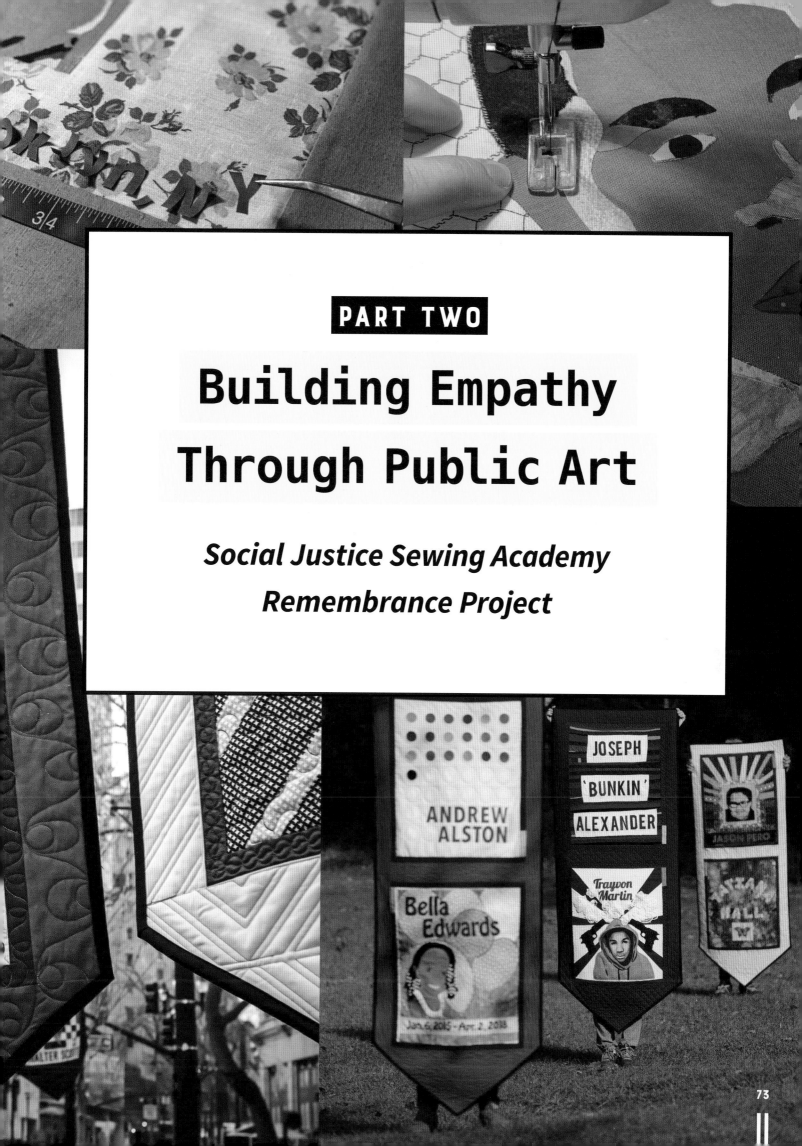

**PART TWO**

# Building Empathy Through Public Art

*Social Justice Sewing Academy Remembrance Project*

## IN ESSENCE, THE SOCIAL JUSTICE SEWING ACADEMY (SJSA) REMEMBRANCE PROJECT IS A TWENTY-FIRST-CENTURY SEWING CIRCLE.

One stitch at a time, volunteer artists, sewists, quilters, embroiderers, and even people completely unfamiliar with textile art are inspired to create activist art. They are connected only by their desire to stimulate change, force conversation, and reckon with the uncomfortable issue of the systemic racism that is so prevalent in our society. And unlike the sewing circles that sprouted in cozy living rooms 150 years ago, these circles are virtual. Activist remembrance blocks are being created in cities and suburbs, in living rooms and garages, in elaborate sewing studios and tiny sections of kitchen counters. The output is shared online, and ultimately, the banners are displayed in public.

One goal of the Remembrance Project is to match the name of a victim with a volunteer who lives within a few miles of where the person was murdered. Therefore, volunteers are asked to research public information on the life that was stolen. Murder victims honored in the Remembrance Project fall into several categories:

**AUTHORITY** (police, security guard, prison guard, …)

**COMMUNITY** (victim of gangs, neighborhood, …)

**RACE** (racially motivated murder)

**GENDER** (LGBTQI+, domestic violence, …)

On the banners throughout this book, notice the narrow dark sashing strips that surround each block and find one

short colored rectangle of fabric. The color of this fabric signifies the cause of death of the victim, as noted by the four colors listed above.

Makers are asked to create a textile portrait or other display that references the victim's life and honors their memory. In the process, the volunteer is creating a powerful activist symbol, and at the same time, the volunteer is given the opportunity to rediscover and strengthen empathy for their neighbors.

When considering the systemic racism, brutality, gun violence, and violent crime we continue to face today, there are clearly more victims than there are volunteers. George Floyd did not choose to die. He did not want to be a symbol of injustice. His murder has been a reckoning moment in American history and focused attention on accountability. There were countless victims before him, and until it stops, there will be more. The Remembrance Project aims to remind us all to remember these lives that were absolutely stolen. Cut short. Taken from this earth before their time.

While volunteers step up to be a part of this movement, they are helping us heal. At the same time, they are creating a lasting tribute that will ensure we remember these lives. Through the Social Justice Sewing Academy Remembrance Project, we are challenging everyone to do more to value all lives.

These SJSA quilted banners honor the lives of individuals through symbolism and portraiture.

## The First Remembrance Project Block Ever Made: Martha Wolfe

Martha Wolfe walks 2.23 miles a day. Every day. This was not her usual routine, but it is something she started, and committed to, after becoming emotionally invested in the life and death of Ahmaud Arbery.

**Martha has been a volunteer and supporter of SJSA since the beginning.** Initially, back in 2016, she signed up to help coordinate a workshop for a group of high school students that was hosted inside a local fabric store. Martha imagined the project would consume a couple of hours of her time. She ended up dedicating four days to the workshop and has been supporting the work of SJSA ever since.

In June of 2020, Martha was invited to construct the very first block for the Remembrance Project (see Ahmaud Arbery, page 78). She chose to honor the life of Ahmaud Arbery, an unarmed, 25-year-old Black man who was hunted and shot by three armed White men while he was out jogging. Ahmaud was murdered on February 23, 2020, and many people around the United States, adopting 2.23 as a mantra to honor the date he was killed, have taken to jogging, running, or walking 2.23 miles as a symbolic gesture toward the young man who was shot while jogging.

Martha's intricate appliqué portrait is a loving tribute, and she used the full power of her experience as an art quilter to construct a powerful image that depicts a smiling young man with his fingertips gently resting on the rim of his cap. Martha's portrait is so finely detailed, with nuanced skin colors, it is hard to imagine it was constructed from fabric and thread. It is a stunning textile portrait that set the stage for hundreds, even thousands, of volunteers to follow.

Some SJSA remembrance blocks feature intricate portraits made from fabric by quiltmakers who employ sophisticated textile skills.

While she so beautifully captured Ahmaud while he was at the peak of his young life, she felt a deep connection to the sense of loss his family and friends feel, especially his mother. As a mother herself, Martha knows all mothers feel a deep, innate bond to their children. She knows that Ahmaud had a group of people surrounding him that wanted the best for him. They shared his dreams and the aspirations for his future. And Martha has since connected with some of the individuals who host social media accounts in honor of Ahmaud, or "Maud," as his friends called him.

Volunteering has been a part of Martha's routine for most of her adult life. She has joined numerous social causes and supported a myriad of community and mental health issues. She believes the SJSA Remembrance Project is uniquely positioned to achieve two things. First, it honors the lives of so many individuals who have been senselessly killed. Through fabric art, their names, faces, and stories will be forever preserved. But second, and equally important, this project is connecting thousands of makers and viewers to the plight of others. In many cases, volunteers are researching public information and learning the hardships of people of color in order to bring insight and perspective to their art. And for some volunteers who live, work, and worship in mostly White communities, this may be their most meaningful encounter with a person of color.

Not all the names of those being honored in the Remembrance Project have made headlines the way Ahmaud's death did, and that is part of the intent of this effort. Some killings have taken place with little or no attention by the media, neighbors, or elected officials. The facts of these deaths are tragic, but SJSA hopes that by honoring these individuals, their stories will not be forgotten. For Martha, making this block made the tragedy feel real and closer to home. **She wants others to know that they too can be moved to make a difference when they step up and become personally connected to the life story of someone who has died.** And like Martha, they may even find themselves taking an active role in commemorating the circumstances under which they were killed, even if it means walking 2.23 miles every day, without fail.

## Ahmaud Arbery's Life Was Stolen
## in Brunswick, Georgia, in 2020

"Ahmaud Arbery was a 25-year-old Black man from Brunswick, Georgia. On February 23, 2020, he went out for a run. A hateful father (a local retired officer and detective) and his son followed him in their pickup truck and, along with another man in a truck (who videotaped the entire thing), tried to block his run and corner him. When they finally succeeded, they antagonized him and then shot him three times, killing him. Caught on video, the son proceeded to kick Ahmaud's body and call him a racist slur as he lay dying. The horror of this scene sparks outrage and heartbreak in me, as a mother, as a human being.

"But it goes on. Police, prepared to arrest the father, son, and third male at the scene, are directed by the district attorney to make no arrests. Instead, they go to Ahmaud's mother and tell her her son has been killed by a homeowner while he was caught burglarizing their house. This is February 23rd. It is not until the beginning of May that there is a real break in this crime, when a copy of the video of his death is leaked to a radio station and spreads virally. **It is only then, after 74 days, that the perpetrators of the crime are arrested.** And as I am writing this, all three were indicted in Ahmaud's death, just yesterday! If there were no video, would there have been any justice in this crime?

"And now I am sitting with you and remembering you, as a mother would. You were born on the day before my youngest son's birthday. You were working to figure out what you would do with your life. You had a family that cared about you and loves you. You have friends and mentors that are witness to your good life. Your life mattered. I will remember that." ■ MARTHA WOLFE, MAKER

# Robert Sandifer's Life Was Stolen
## in Chicago, Illinois, in 1994

"Robert 'Yummy' Sandifer made national headlines in 1994 when, at age eleven, he made the cover of *Time* magazine and became the face of a tragic, emerging phenomenon dubbed 'kids killing kids.' He was reputedly a member of a Chicago gang, and in that capacity was alleged to have killed a thirteen-year-old girl. In response, two of his fellow gang members killed Yummy, in an attempt to curtail affiliate liability. Yummy's face and name were splashed across magazines and newspapers in the weeks and months after his murder. **Despite detailing the years of abuse, neglect, and affliction Yummy was subjected to since birth, much of the press coverage nonetheless characterized him in negative, derisive terms.**

"As I worked on this piece honoring Yummy, I thought of eleven-year-old boys I know now, and the comparatively charmed lives they lead. Yummy, in sharp contrast, was born into, and was a product of, socioeconomic hardships. Factors outside his control stranded him. Social welfare systems failed him. Instead of branding him a mini-monster, it is important to consider the cycles of poverty, addiction, abuse, and neglect that impacted and shaped Robert's young character, and to consider the broad-stroke systemic changes we can and must make if we are to interrupt these vicious cycles.

"In creating this banner honoring Yummy, I wanted to express that despite the harsh characterizations of him as a ne'er-do-well, a gang thug, a murderer, Robert Sandifer was a tiny, eleven-year-old boy from Chicago who got his nickname because he loved cookies. What became of him rests on all our shoulders.

"*Personal note:* I first met Robert Sandifer in late 1993, at which time I was one of his attorneys in family court proceedings. As such, I count myself as part of the system that failed him.

"Over 25 years later, I sit stitching a banner honoring Yummy as part of the Social Justice Sewing Academy's Remembrance Project. Revisiting the story of Robert's brief life has been a disheartening experience. What progress has been made to change the path of so many born into circumstances similar to his?"

▦ ANN O'CALLAGHAN SHOUP, MAKER

## Trayvon Martin's Life Was Stolen
## in Sanford, Florida, in 2012

"We wept. Black people collectively mourned the loss of Trayvon Martin because in his death we saw our own sons' experience in this country reflected. Their too-brief childhoods lived under a constant threat of violence. Violence that works to snuff out the flame that illuminates the beauty, joy, and spirit in being a Black boy. We remembered how, when the individual vigilantes weren't enough, this country built institutions, cited policies, and wrote laws to extend their reach in the murdering of our sons. And how even that wasn't enough to diminish the light, because it will never be enough, because Black boys in life and even in death will always shine.

"Trayvon taught us that. We held tight. We understood in intimate detail how the justice system works to dehumanize our sons, our brothers, our fathers, because we had seen it countless times before. We knew that no one but us could protect our sons because no one but us saw the true value in their lives—our whole ancestry in their eyes and the whole universe in their smile. While the system continued to uphold white supremacy and anti-blackness, Black people searched for hope. A tiny flickering deep within our bellies very nearly extinguished by our tears. We tended those embers until they glowed bright white with heat. It fueled us and propelled us forward with the strength to demand from this country what they told us was impossible. Trayvon prepared us for that. We exhaled. We lit a raging fire to honor our beloved Trayvon. A fire so bright that no one could look away from our tear-stained faces lest they be burned by the flames. We wouldn't let them martyr our son and boil his life down to his last few breaths. **He inspired us to take to the streets, to organize, and to lean on our collective strength.** He was a reminder for us to look to our ancestors and turn our collective trauma into action. From the Black Lives Matter movement to the Social Justice Sewing Academy, we were able to create spaces that honored his life and the lives of all our loved ones taken too soon. Trayvon is our son and our brother, our past and our future. He is a reminder to hold tight to our Black sons, to revel in their joy, to love and protect them from a world too small to see their greatness."

■ ASIJA CHAPPEL WUORENMAA, MAKER

# Clementa Pinckney's Life Was Stolen
## in Charleston, South Carolina, in 2015

"I made this block in honor of former South Carolina Senator and ReverendClementa Carlos Pinckney. Born July 30, 1973, in Beaufort, South Carolina, Clementa Pinckney began preaching at his home church, St. John African Methodist Episcopal (AME) Church in Ridgeland, South Carolina, at the age of thirteen. At eighteen he became a pastor, and by 2010 he was leading the historic Mother Emanuel AME Church in Charleston, where on June 17, 2015, while leading a Bible study group, he was killed, along with eight others, by a hate-filled 21-year-old white supremacist hoping to incite a race war.

**"Clementa Pinckney was devoted to his church, family, and community.** In 1996, at 23, he was the youngest African American elected to the South Carolina General Assembly, and he went on to serve as a state senator from 2001 until his death. Rev. Pinckney was a born leader; the list of his accolades and achievements is long. While attending Jasper County High School, he was elected class president for two years. He graduated magna cum laude with a bachelor of arts degree from Allen University in 1995, while also serving as freshman class president, student body president, and senior class president; and in his junior year, he received a Woodrow Wilson Research Fellowship for summer study at Princeton University in the fields of public policy and international affairs. In 1999, after having been awarded a graduate fellowship, he received a master of public administration degree from the University of South Carolina. He went on to receive a master of divinity degree from Lutheran Theological Southern Seminary and, at the time of his death, was a student at Wesley Theological Seminary pursuing a doctor of ministry degree, which was awarded posthumously in 2016. His wife, Jennifer, and daughters, Eliana and Malana, accepted the diploma and hood that symbolized his achievement. He is remembered by his family, friends, and colleagues as noble, humble, genuine, patient, intelligent, passionate, profound, kind, dedicated, and selfless.

"While designing this piece to honor Clementa Pinckney, I chose to represent the main arch and stained glass of Mother Emanuel Church as the central theme because faith was central to Rev. Pinckney's life. Below his name are two blocks that quilters will recognize as the Courthouse Steps pattern, symbolizing his service in government. On March 24, 2018, his wife and daughters spoke at a March for Our Lives rally in front of the South Carolina State House. As a personal tribute, they and friend and fellow senator Gerald Malloy were each wearing one of Clementa's baseball caps. The cap on this block is there to remind us that, in addition to all his achievements, he was one of us too. In the words of President Obama eulogizing Pinckney, 'What a good man.'"

■ KATHY MORGANROTH, MAKER

## Michael Brown's Life Was Stolen
### in Ferguson, Missouri, in 2014

"In honor of Michael Brown (1996–2014), an unarmed, eighteen-year-old young man who loved rap music, video games, and hanging out with friends. He had just graduated from high school with plans to attend college in a few weeks when he was shot six times and killed by a police officer. Weeks before his death, while looking at after-storm clouds, Michael called his father to say that he had seen an angel in them, being chased by Satan and running into the face of God. 'Now I believe,' he said. **Michael Brown was a young man with hopes and an openness to the wonders in this world.** Stitched with a mama's heart."
■ HAZEL C. MONTE, MAKER

## Dawn Boyd's Life Was Stolen
### in West Philadelphia, Pennsylvania, in 2017

"Dawn Boyd was sitting outside with her friends and their infant children when she and three others were struck by gunfire from a passing car. Dawn and one of her friends died as a result. Dawn's daughter and her friend's son were not injured, and Dawn is credited with saving their lives. Family members shared that Dawn shielded her baby from the bullets, then grabbed both babies and tried to get them inside to safety.

"Dawn turned 22 just a few days before she was killed. She is missed by her friends and large family who called her Sissy. Family members shared that her baby, Sameya, was her top priority in life and being a mother was the role that she cherished the most. **She is remembered for her 'infectious laugh and ready smile.'** Dawn was one of 353 victims of homicide in Philadelphia in 2018. She was another victim of gun violence in Philadelphia and a victim of the failure of the state of Pennsylvania to enact commonsense gun laws and reforms. I used Dawn's name as the inspiration for the design of this block. The young lives that she saved are represented by the two flowers in bloom." ■ REBECCA THUT WITMER, MAKER

## Nicholas Bils's Life Was Stolen
### in San Diego, California, in 2020

"The story of how Nicholas Bils was shot is difficult to read. It was such a badly managed situation. The park rangers who had captured Nicholas did not secure him well in their vehicle. Nicholas escaped right outside of the San Diego Central Jail and was shot in the back by another officer who just happened to be there when he ran. **Nicholas had schizophrenia and was carrying no weapon.** He was in the vehicle for putting golf balls in a closed park with his dog off leash, hardly a reason to kill a man. I had no idea it had happened, although it was here in my county.

"The officer who shot and killed Nicholas has been charged, but I haven't seen results from that yet. I did spend time watching videos of Nicholas's mom and brother talking about him, and their love and care for him was so obvious, so I added the hearts watching over him. His dog was an important part of his life, and though I couldn't find a picture of it, I found its name was either Rio or River, so I added a generic dog and a river to the background. I hope we can find a way to better handle mental illness across the board, but training the police not to shoot first and ask later would be a start." ■ KATHY NIDA, MAKER

## Taliesin Myrddin Namkai—Meche's Life Was Stolen
## in Portland, Oregon, in 2016

"When given the now-familiar-to-me name of Taliesin Myrddin Namkai-Meche, I was both set at ease and felt an odd weight of responsibility. In a project designed to highlight and raise up individuals who have lost their lives unjustly, due to racially motivated violence, I figure a middle-class, White male (whose killer was quickly apprehended and granted a trial) is an anomaly. That said, Taliesin gave his life standing up, with two others, to shield two young women of color who were being verbally assaulted with racist and Islamophobic slurs while riding public transit in Portland, Oregon.

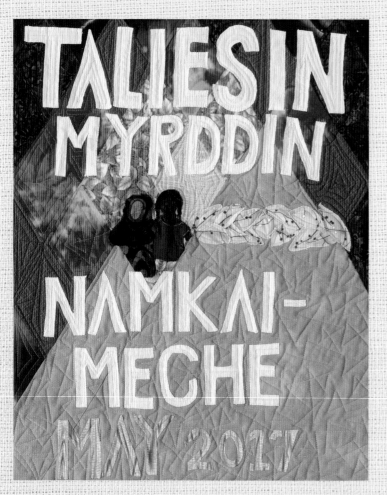

**"From everything I've read, he valued peace and felt strongly about supporting all those around him.** He supposedly greeted all with a huge smile and an inner light, and seeing an injustice, he would not let it pass without speaking up. It seems he lived his short life of 23 years embodying the character his parents knew to be part of his being when they first gave him a name steeped in symbolism and spiritual mysticism. According to one article I found, he was named after the sixth-century Welsh bard and shaman Taliesin, a name that also means 'shining brow.' His middle name is a wizard's name, Myrddin, which in Arthurian legend became Merlin. And when his mother, Asha, was pregnant with Taliesin, his father, Christopher, dreamed that his son was coming as a flame from the heavens. For the child's last name, a rinpoche gave them Namkai-Meche, which means 'a flame from the sky.'

"The background for this remembrance block illustrates a 'flame from the sky' set as the backdrop for mountain peaks from the Cascade Range in Oregon (he was an Oregon native and an avid hiker and backpacker). The golden laurel wreath not only plays off of the meaning of his first name but is a representation of an actual crown of gold he is pictured with in his college graduation photos in cap and gown as well as other photos of him while hiking with friends. The figures in the center are the two girls whose safety was of his utmost concern in his last moments, who may themselves have been victims of violence had Taliesin and the other two brave souls not intervened. May their act of bravery and selflessness remain a shining light." ■ **LINDA NUSSBAUM, MAKER**

## Vanessa Guillén's Life Was Stolen in Fort Hood, Texas, in 2020

"Vanessa Guillén was a twenty-year-old Army specialist from Texas. She was murdered by another service member, who her family says had been harassing her. As the spouse of a twenty-year Army vet, and as a woman, it pains me to know that the military system of reporting abuse has long been insufficient and attempts to improve it have been passed over. **Vanessa was too young, with too much potential and too much love for life and service, to have been taken from this world.** My block attempts to honor her vibrancy, her service in the Army, and her proud Hispanic heritage. May her memory be a blessing to her 'family.' "

■ **KRISTIN LA FLAMME, MAKER**

## Amadou Diallo's Life Was Stolen in New York, New York, in 1999

"It was an honor to be asked to join in on such a special project. **My only wish is that this project didn't exist because that would mean things like this were not happening in our country.** I hope that when Amadou Diallo's family sees this block it will bring comfort and that it will inspire others to research his name and support the foundation his mother has set in place in his memory."

■ **SUMMER SWANSON, MAKER**

## Srinivas Kuchibhotla's Life Was Stolen
## in Olathe, Kansas, in 2017

" 'Do we belong here?' Sunayana Dumala, the grief-stricken wife of Srinivas Kuchibhotla, asked following the death of her beloved husband. Their life and dreams for an American future together had just been shattered. Mr. Kuchibhotla was killed in a racially motivated hate crime. The gunman had yelled, 'Get out of my country!,' and pulled the trigger. An immigrant from India, Mr. Kuchibhotla was an aviation engineer at Garmin, headquartered in Olathe, Kansas. He had graduated from the University of Texas, El Paso. Coming to the U.S. to pursue a postgraduate degree is an outcome of determination and hard work, and oftentimes is monetarily made possible by the life savings of selfless parents. Arriving here is the first miracle and making a life here away from loved ones is the other. **All of this was wiped out by one man's rejection of Mr. Kuchibhotla and what America stands for.** The answer to Sunayana Dumala's question, 'Do we belong here?,' is an emphatic *'Yes, we belong!'* " ■ JOVITA REVATHI VAS, MAKER

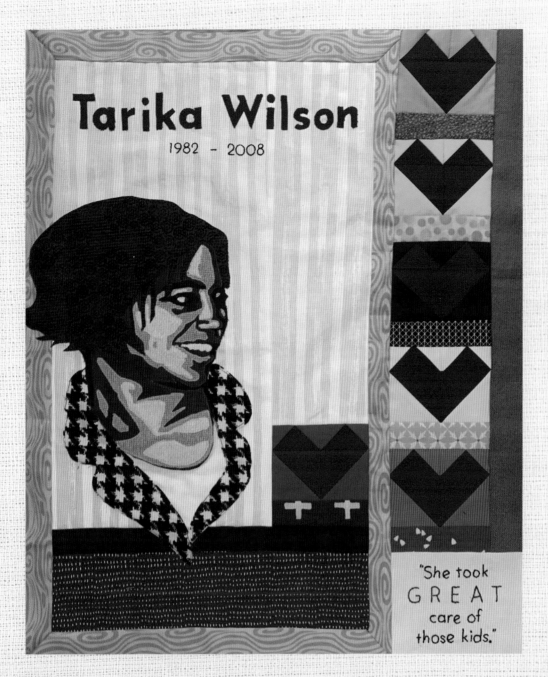

## Tarika Wilson's Life Was Stolen
## in Lima, Ohio, in 2008

"Tarika Wilson was shot and killed by the police in Lima, Ohio, at age 26. She was hiding in a bedroom protecting her six small children when the police entered her boyfriend's house to execute a warrant that did not include her. One officer shot at her boyfriend's dog, and a second officer heard the shots and reacted by shooting blindly through the bedroom door. Tarika was killed, and her one-year-old baby, who was in her arms, sustained injuries.

**"Making this block was a heartbreaking privilege.** The six hearts represent her six children (between the ages of one and eight when she was murdered). There weren't a lot of public photos available to reference, but one that I found showed Tarika holding a baby and smiling at him. I used that as my main reference for her face, because it showed how young she was and captured the love and joy she felt for her children. My dad and I worked together on creating the portrait.... He did the drawings and I created it with fabric. I used the wood-grain fabric to create the suggestion of a door frame, and the words I embroidered, 'She took great care of those kids,' are part of a quote from her uncle after her death. The officer who murdered Tarika was acquitted of all charges by an all-White jury." ■ JOANNA MALACHOWSKY, MAKER

## Oluwatoyin Salau's Life Was Stolen in Tallahassee, Florida, in 2020

"Oluwatoyin 'Toyin' Salau committed her life to fighting injustice for all Black lives as she worked to survive in a world that works aggressively to harm, silence, and kill Black women. **Toyin's experience speaks the unspeakable—that one in four Black girls are survivors of sexual abuse, that one in five Black women are the survivors of rape, and that Black women are more likely to experience sexual violence than their White, Asian, and Latina peers.** This block is dedicated to Toyin and to all Black girls—those who have passed on and those still living—who have buried their dreams, their hopes, and their voices in graves. Rest in peace, Oluwatoyin." ■ ASIJA CHAPPEL WUORENMAA, MAKER

## Michelle Simone "Tamika" Washington's Life Was Stolen in Philadelphia, Pennsylvania, in 2019

"This block remembers and honors Michelle 'Tamika' Washington, also known as Michelle Simone in the LGBTQI+ community, a 40-year-old Philadelphia resident, murdered on May 19, 2019. Michelle tragically became the third Black transgender woman killed by violence in a short period of 2019, and the fifth transgender woman of color known to be killed by gun violence in 2019. Michelle Simone studied nursing and was known as an outspoken advocate in her local community. **Newspaper articles include quotes from friends describing her as a 'trailblazer, caregiver, a nurturer' and an 'auntie to the community.'** With the creation of this block, I hope to honor the memory of Michelle, and advocate to protect trans lives. Using a combination of paint and textiles, and inspired by social media photos of Michelle, I chose a color palette of purples for her portrait and included florals to represent her nurturing spirit. Her work and her life will not be forgotten." ■ LACI HESS, MAKER

# Lexi "Ebony" Sutton's Life Was Stolen
## in Harlem, New York, in 2020

"Lexi 'Ebony' Sutton was a transgender, nonconforming person who was murdered March 28, 2020, in Harlem, New York. She also went by the name Lexus Knockzema Ebony Sutton. They loved music, poetry, makeup, fashion, and dancing. Lexi also liked to rap under the name Lil' Killer. They were into dance styles called twisting and voguing, and possibly appeared as a dancer in the ballroom scene with the Legendary Iconic House of Ebony. If you have ever watched the series *Pose* or the documentary *Paris Is Burning*, you would see this style of dancing. The ballroom scene is all about fashion as well, and it was easy to tell from Lexi's Facebook page that they loved putting looks together. Lexi also loved to watch *RuPaul's Drag Race*, which we both have in common. One of my favorite taglines from the show has always been 'Not today, Satan! Not today!' and I found a photo of Lexi with that saying in the frame, which just made me sob a little. Lexi was a person who I wish I had met. A friend named Lavonia Brooks remembered Lexi as a private and generous person. 'She's very giving. She would give you the shoes off her feet in the wintertime if she really had to,' Brooks said. 'I really looked up to her because of her tolerance and respect. Lexi had a beautiful heart, and she was very gifted.'

"The quilt block I made I titled A Crown for Lexi. I chose bright happy colors for her name because she was such a bright, vivid person. I appliquéd a golden crown for her, to represent the ballroom scene she loved, and embroidered her other name, Lexus Knockzema Ebony, because it just needed to be there. I added border fabric with poetry on it since Lexi loved that. The lettering I used for Lexi's name is a style of bubble letters I used to do as a teen when I wanted to be a graphic designer, and I thought it would add my flair to the block.

**"There is an epidemic of violence against the transgender and nonbinary community, and especially against Black transgender women.** In November 2019, ahead of Transgender Day of Remembrance, the Human Rights Campaign (HRC) Foundation released *A National Epidemic: Fatal Anti-Transgender Violence in the United States in 2019*, a heartbreaking report honoring the trans people killed and detailing the contributing and motivating factors that lead to this tragic violence. Sadly,

2019 saw at least 26 transgender or gender-nonconforming people fatally shot or killed by other violent means. Too often, these stories go unreported or misreported.

"There are currently very few explicit federal legal protections for transgender or gender-expansive people. At the state level, transgender and gender-nonconforming people in New York are explicitly protected in employment, housing, and public spaces, and they are covered under the state's hate crimes legislation. Nationally, despite some marginal gains in state and local policies that support and affirm transgender people, recent years have been marked by anti-LGBTQI+ attacks at all levels of government. **We must demand better from our elected officials and reject harmful anti-transgender legislation appearing at the local, state, and federal levels because it is clear that fatal violence disproportionately affects transgender women of color.** The intersections of racism, transphobia, sexism, biphobia, and homophobia conspire to deprive them of necessities to live and thrive." ■ ANGELIQUE MCGINLEY, MAKER

## Gabriella Nevarez's Life Was Stolen in Sacramento, California, in 2019

"I used a technique learned from a workshop with Timna Tarr, using double-sided fusible web, which I ironed to a background fabric, then stitched down. I used Robert Kaufman Fresh Hues Ombre Earth for Gabby's face, hands, and shoulders. Gabby's shirt, hair, and letters are made with a mix of batik fabrics. I used Giucy Giuce Quantum Fabric for the background and border, a choice I now regret, as I have realized that Andover Fabrics has been stunningly silent on the BLM movement. I had researched the fabric designer Giucy Giuce but failed to look at Andover before choosing this line. I'm sorry it's too late to go back on this fabric choice and vow to be more careful in the future. I made this block while listening to *The New Jim Crow* by Michelle Alexander to help further my learning of policing and imprisonment practices and policies. **Gabby's case is related to mental health and inappropriately escalated police responses.**" ■ TAMLIN MATTHEWS, MAKER

## Sierra Robinson's and Noelani Robinson's Lives Were Stolen in Milwaukee, Wisconsin, in 2019

"Sierra Robinson, a beautiful young mother who loved make-up and reading poetry, and her young daughter, Noelani, died together in a terrible act of violence. Sierra spoke about wanting to write a book about her life. **Sadly, we will never get to read that book, or find out what she would have made of her life.** To me, that is a profoundly sad thing, but I'm glad that I had the opportunity to find out a little about her and to memorialize her, along with her daughter." ■ TOBY SCHWARTZ, MAKER

## Tianya Gaddis's Life Was Stolen
## in Oakland, California, in 2014

"On March 1, 2014, Tianya Gaddis was hanging out with friends in Oakland, California, when she was struck by at least one bullet. She died three hours later. Whether she was an intended target or hit by a stray bullet, her murder was never solved. Tianya was 25 at the time of her death. She was survived by a daughter in grade school, plus many friends and family members.

"Aside from two paragraphs in local papers about homicides, Tianya's death received no media coverage. Everything I learned about her was from her sister's Instagram account. **It was heartbreaking to find that the family lost not only Tianya, but also her brother and her cousin, to gun violence in the following three years.** I keenly felt the divide between the circumstances of my life where, due to skin color, structural American racism, and socioeconomic situation, I have never lost a friend or family member to gun violence, nor have I ever seen funeral photos posted on my friends' social media accounts.

"The most important goal for me in creating this remembrance of Tianya was to make sure it represented her as a vibrant human being. I chose this photo because she looked happy and ready to carry on with all that life was offering her. In the context of the block, she is perhaps looking back at us as she goes to a better place. Her sister often wrote 'Rest in Paradise' on posts about Tianya. I wanted the words around her head to have a halo-like effect. Her sister used the phrase 'Always So Focused' in one post about Tianya, and that felt important to include, as Tianya worked in health care, was raising her daughter, and also had an active social life with friends and family. She was a successful person by the standards of American society, and she deserved all that life had to offer. It breaks my heart to think how much life she still had to live and how much time was stolen from her

and her daughter. My own mother is 77 and I am 50, and I can't begin to imagine what life would be like if my mom had been taken so early and so violently.

"I hope her family and friends are happy with this block for Tianya. While the responsibility has often felt overwhelming, it has been a privilege to learn about Tianya and create her remembrance block. While I was making it, I thought constantly about what this block would mean and how it was an opportunity for Tianya to be represented in a nationwide reckoning with an American epidemic. Many thanks to SJSA for creating and facilitating this project." ■ LOZ LOORY, MAKER

## Amaria Jones's Life Was Stolen
## in Chicago, Illinois, in 2020

"Amaria Jones was thirteen when she was shot in the neck while dancing in her living room. She bled to death in front of her mother from a bullet that went through her TV and a 'Chicago Lives Matter' poster in her window. She was among 104 other people shot in Chicago on the weekend of Father's Day, 2020.

**"She was a dancer, a basketball player, a sister, a daughter, a friend.** She wanted to become a lawyer. Her favorite color was purple. My son's favorite color is purple. We love dancing in our living room. My husband is a lawyer. My nephews play basketball. Our families are both from Chicago. Her family thinks of others in their time of grief. That is where we start to differ. Amaria Jones. Say her name.

"The background of her block is her favorite color, the same color as her casket. Her hands are pictured at the top in a sign of love. She is depicted as the dancer in the middle. She is lying on top of 104 individually cut pieces of fabric to represent the other victims of gun violence that weekend in Chicago. The squares are intertwined, and one could not be moved without moving the others. Their edges are left raw and unsecured, like the victims and their families. They will continue to fray over time. Their shape is imprecise to depict the chaos left in the wake of gun violence. Amaria Jones. Say her name." ■ MELISSA DODD, MAKER

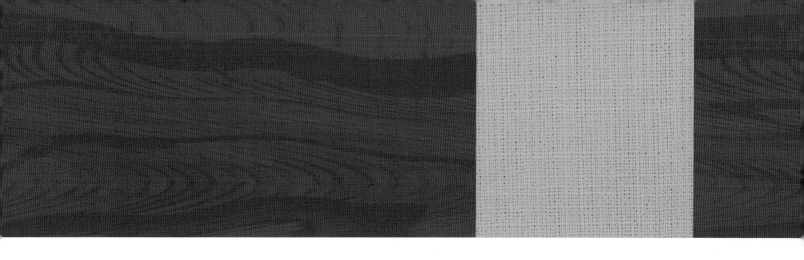

# A. J. Jones's Life Was Stolen
## in Newark, New Jersey, in 2018

"A. J. Jones was born on December 7, 1998, the only son to his mother, Trina Jones. A. J., short for Amazing Joy, would have been celebrating his 22nd birthday this December, had his life not been senselessly cut short after he was robbed in Newark, New Jersey, in July of 2018. Reportedly he used his dying breaths to encourage a close friend, shot alongside him, to cling to life. His friend survived, but A. J. lives on only in memory.

"In my search to learn more about A. J.'s life, I found details online, both big and small. A. J. was left-handed, quick-witted, and an enthusiastic but terrible dancer. His friends called him 'Kickup.' **He tested as gifted at a very young age and demonstrated warmth and empathy for others far beyond his years.** Much of what I found was authored by Trina, who became his voice in death, speaking out in search of justice for her son. She recorded an episode of the podcast *Through Her Eyes* in which she laid bare the details of A. J.'s murder, of what it was like to have her entire world shattered after her only son was ripped from her. Trina's agony is palpable. At one point, she recalled an overwhelming compulsion to bring blankets to the morgue, such was her grief and worry that her son would be cold as he lay alone on the examination table. Out of all the heartbreaking details of A. J.'s death, this I just can't shake.

"A. J. was exploring his passion for music prior to his death—writing and recording at a local studio. To honor him in this block, I thought about the life and career he might have had. Inspired by the work of a letterpress concert poster producer whose operations I visited last year, I designed what a poster for one of A. J.'s shows might have looked like. I wanted to capture the smile his mother loved so dearly. The many layers of fabric proved challenging to wrangle, and after all the attention I spent on A. J.'s face to depict him as accurately as possible, the detail of the folds in his shirt was tempting to crop out or simplify. But the more I looked at them, the more they reminded me of the folds in an armful of blankets, grabbed in haste by a mother in the throes of grief, rushing to care for her beloved son." ■ **AMANDA COLYER, MAKER**

## Sean Adler's Life Was Stolen
## in Los Angeles, California, in 2018

"Sean Adler, age 48, was murdered on November 7, 2018, during a mass shooting at Borderline Bar and Grill in Thousand Oaks, California. Those who survived the massacre say that Mr. Adler sacrificed his life to save others, and he is honored and remembered as a hero that night. He was also a devoted husband and a wonderful father to his two sons, ages seventeen and twelve, at the time of his death. He was a loving man to friends and neighbors, and a coffee lover.

"Mr. Adler had recently achieved his dream of opening a coffee shop in Simi Valley just three weeks before his life was taken by a domestic terrorist. **Mr. Adler worked hard all his life and loved and supported others with his kindness and his actions.** It is clear from all that has been published about him since his death that he was a positive, helpful, and kind person.

"The block is composed of several representations of Mr. Adler. For his love of Hawaiian shirts, which all who attended his funeral service wore, there are three shirts to represent his wife and two sons. There is a fist, which was the symbol for his coffee shop, Rivalry Roasters, alongside abstract art representations of coffee beans (brown) and the coffee plant (green). The heart is composed of the same fabric as the Hawaiian shirts, to represent his love for his family, his love for the people in his life, and the ultimate show of love for the people he saved when he attempted to disarm the gunman.

"It was an honor and a privilege to create this block. My heart hurts daily for the many people murdered and for those who must live with such tremendous losses. Fist for Justice paper-pieced pattern by @getupandsew."

◼ DANA STONE, MAKER

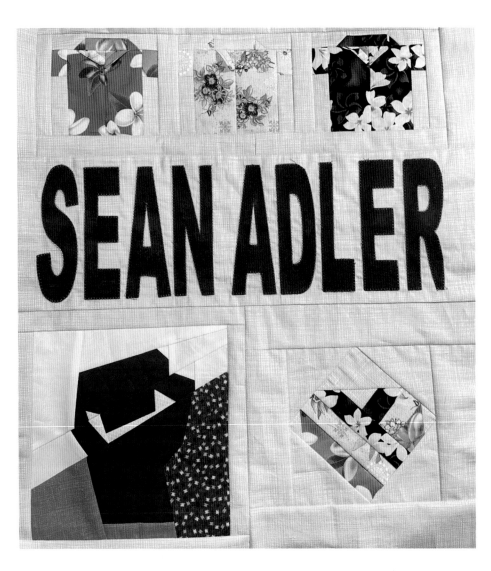

## Rekia Boyd's Life Was Stolen
## in Chicago, Illinois, in 2020

"Rekia Boyd's funeral was held on the day she was scheduled to begin nursing school. While out one night with friends, she was shot in the back of the head by a White, male off-duty police officer who had approached her group in his car. She was 22 years old.

"According to her brother, she made friends wherever she went. Having discovered through my research her favorite color to be yellow, I framed her portrait with every kind of yellow fabric I could find in my collection. I do not know if she liked flowers, but I placed a large yellow one above her head in a symbolic gesture. I wanted to somehow offer a token of beauty and healing energy to the area that received the fatal violence.

"The only complaint that had drawn the off-duty police officer to Rekia's group of friends that night was that they were being loud. In reflection, I think of the hundreds of nights I spent in my early twenties out late on the streets being loud … definitely being loud. Not once was I ever verbally or physically harassed by police …

but I am White and most of my friends were White. **It is my hope that in honoring the lives of these individuals through the quilts made for the Remembrance Project, awareness will be raised regarding the systemic racism and racially motivated violence that has prevailed since this country's inception.** The case against Dante Servin in Rekia Boyd's death illuminates the perpetual injustice suffered through the disturbing irony whereby the judge dismissed the case, stating that instead of being charged with involuntary manslaughter, he should have been charged with first-degree murder—allowing Dante Servin, in the end, to get away with murder.

"Out of the handful of photographs of Rekia Boyd, I chose the one where her head is tilted down while her eyes are looking up with a direct gaze, making her appear all-knowing." ■ NIKA FELDMAN, MAKER

## Eleanor Bumpurs's Life Was Stolen in Bronx, New York, in 1984

"Eleanor Bumpurs was born in 1918 in North Carolina. She was the only girl of six children, and at age nine, when her mother died, she was taken out of school to help around the house. **Bumpurs came of age in the Jim Crow South and eventually moved to New York.** Bumpurs had seven children from various romantic unions but was ultimately a single mom. Bumpurs is said to have loved cooking for her family. In a 2017 interview, Mary Bumpurs, reminiscing about her mother's cooking skills, said, 'We were poor, but she always fed her children. Her cooking was so good. No store-bought food. Everything was from scratch. She could make water smell good.'

"In her 60s, Bumpurs had started to develop serious mental health issues. In 1984, she stopped paying her $80 monthly rent, because she maintained that 'Ronald Reagan and his people had come through the walls.' The New York housing authorities planned to evict Bumpurs and relocate her to a medical facility. On October 29, 1984, NYPD arrived at Bumpurs's apartment to proceed with the eviction and broke her door down. Bumpurs picked up a kitchen knife, and officer Stephen Sullivan, armed with a shotgun, shot her twice, ultimately ending her life." ■ **MADDIE PESAVENTO, MAKER**

## Jason Washington's Life Was Stolen in Portland, Oregon, in 2018

"When I received Jason Washington's name and information, I recalled with great sadness hearing about his death. I remembered when it happened because it happened here in the city in which I live. What struck me most about Jason was the things he had in common with my husband, such as having served in the Navy and the U.S. Postal Service. I could so easily imagine him being buddies with my husband. In his photos he always looked so friendly and easygoing. I bet he had a great laugh. **I know he was a good friend because he died while actually trying to prevent his friend from getting into trouble.** May you rest in peace, Jason Washington, and may your loved ones always remember your love and your loyalty."
■ **LULU MOONWOOD MURAKAMI, MAKER**

# Alaina Petty's Life Was Stolen
# in Parkland, Florida in, 2018

"Alaina Petty, age fourteen. 'It's hard to be a girl today. There's so much pressure from everyone to dress and act a certain way to be liked and popular, but none of that seemed to affect Alaina. She was always sticking up for other people and for herself,' Alaina's big sister, Meghan, said. People described her as super funny, kind, sassy, and determined. But what really got me was the way she befriended people, how her nonjudgmental attitude allowed her to make friends quickly and keep them.

"The quilt features the Everglades—she loved the way nature and being outside made her feel. Her school was named for an early Everglades conservationist, Marjory Stoneman Douglas. It also includes a mangrove—those trees that manage to thrive and survive where fresh water meets salt water, with their roots exposed to the elements, protecting shorelines and wildlife from storms and hurricanes. **The heart of this very specific ecosystem captured a lot of the qualities Alaina's friends and family attributed to her.**

"The Bayahíbe rose is the national flower of the Dominican Republic, a nod to Alaina's love of Bachata, Spanish, and Latin pop. In the water flowing through the roots, I included symbols of things that were important to her or that reveal some of who she was: her dogs, a flag for her love for her country and the Junior ROTC program, where she excelled. Her teacher said, 'She was pleasantly aggressive. But her drive wasn't selfish; it was kind of like "Let's all be better together."' The Mormon helping hands are for her faith and the way she loved doing community service projects. The four bubbles are

for her place among her siblings, with whom she was very close. The chopsticks are for her love of ramen, and the mountain is for the state of Washington, where she spent the first ten years of her life. Alaina was a victim of one of the deadliest school shootings in U.S. history, on February 14, 2018, in Parkland, Florida. But in reading all that's been written about her since her death, I can't help but feel amazed at the impact of her short life. Rest in power, you sweet girl." ■ JULIE BOWDEN, MAKER

## Bella Edwards's Life Was Stolen
## in Queens, New York, in 2018

"Bella Edwards, whose mother described her as 'friendly, beautiful, affectionate, and smart,' was only three years old when she died from injuries inflicted on her young body by her mother's boyfriend, a man who had previously been tried, convicted, and served time for another violent crime. It's difficult to write a tribute for such a young child. What accomplishments can we acknowledge when she was really just at the beginning of being the person she was meant to become? Perhaps she'd recently mastered walking up and down stairs using one foot on each step or was proud of getting dressed each morning all by herself. Maybe she was learning her alphabet or delighted everyone by singing with perfect pitch? **We don't know what exciting little victories she could have been celebrating every day.**

"In my block, I tried to capture Bella's bright smile, sparkling eyes, and something of her loving spirit. The round shapes represent the balloons that were present two days after her death when friends and family gathered for a candlelight vigil. The loss of her innocent life and the brutal manner of her death are difficult to contemplate—I find myself wondering, how many adults are to blame, how many systems failed to protect this child? Was the world robbed of a brilliant doctor, a warm and caring teacher, or maybe an architect? Was she destined to be an artist, a judge, or maybe a poet? We'll never know." ■ **KENDRA J. DOWD, MAKER**

# Shelly Frey's Life Was Stolen
## in Houston, Texas, in 2012

"Shelly Frey was a 27-year-old mother, daughter, and friend. Her mother, Sharon Wilkerson, said, 'She wanted to show women that they were beautiful, they were going to be somebody. Her dream was to help others.' On December 6, 2012, Shelly Frey and a friend were murdered by Louis Campbell, an off-duty sheriff's deputy in Houston, Texas. She was shopping at Walmart with two friends and two small children. The off-duty sheriff's deputy allegedly thought they were shoplifting, so he followed them out of the store and to their car. Supposedly, he felt like his life was in danger when they started to drive off, so he shot into the car with the three women and two children inside. Shelly Frey, a passenger in the car, was shot twice in the neck and died from gunshot wounds. Louis Campbell has not faced any charges.

"Shelly Frey was a Hurricane Katrina survivor. She moved to Houston to start a new life with her two children. Her daughter suffered from sickle cell anemia, so it was hard to maintain a steady job. She did the best that she could with what she was given. She was described as a fashionista and was always smiling. When researching her, I realized that I had not heard her story. So I had to dig deep and read between the headlines that tried to criminalize her with mistakes she'd made in the past.

**Her mistakes are not who she was, and they don't justify her murder.** Remember her and say her name.

"The kites and diamond shapes can be interpreted as following your dreams and flying high. Shelly's circumstances led her to Houston, where, if she had the precious time that was taken from her, she would have flown high above the clouds. Like a diamond, Shelly was beautiful, precious, and rare." ■ **ALICIA MARCHA, MAKER**

"Hug your Black daughter extra tight tonight, because the world outside your arms will literally discard her and then say it was her fault."
■ JAMILAH LEMIEUX

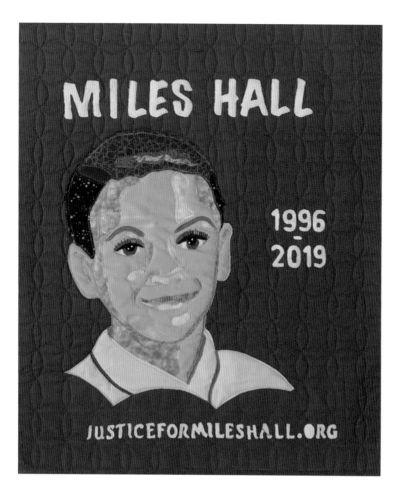

## Miles Hall's Life Was Stolen in Walnut Creek, California, in 2019

"Searching through photos of Miles, his life, and his family at justiceformileshall.org, I was struck by his large, bright, captivating eyes—especially those beautiful, long lashes that defied reality. **I wished to capture his eyes and the light that sparkled through his little-boy gaze in his school portrait—the familiar photo setting that is recognizable for millions of little boys during those sweet elementary school years.** As a mom of a son that turned 23 years old the week I began to work on this tribute (the same age as Miles at his death), I held Miles's family closely in my heart—especially his mother—with hopes that I might properly honor him by capturing his essence and spirit through the light in his beautiful eyes."

■ LORRAINE WOODRUFF-LONG, MAKER

## Kayla Moore's Life Was Stolen in Berkeley, California, in 2013

"Kayla Moore was born Xavier Moore on April 17, 1971, and died at age 41 on February 13, 2013. She was a beloved daughter, sister, auntie, and friend. **She was intelligent, generous to her friends, and a talented singer, dancer, and poet.** She was the life of every party. She had many challenges, but was committed to being herself starting at age twelve. She was a transgender Black woman, diagnosed with paranoid schizophrenia, intrinsic cardiovascular disease, and obesity. On the day she died, she had a psychotic episode combined with drugs, alcohol, police (not following all procedures), and an invalid warrant for her arrest: a lethal combination. Kayla had the soul of a poet and had things yet to say." ■ DENISE OYAMA MILLER, MAKER

# Valente Acosta–Bustillos's Life Was Stolen
## in Albuquerque, New Mexico, in 2020

"When I was assigned Valente Acosta-Bustillos's name for a remembrance block, I easily found new stories detailing his death, although I wanted his block to represent his life. I was fortunate to come across his family's remembrance page on the local mortuary's website. In their description and in the photos, I was able to get a good picture of who he was as a man, and what was important to him: family, faith, heritage, work. I tried to represent these qualities in the block.

"In terms of the design, the idea of the *papel picado* (perforated paper) came first. It's often used in Día de los Muertos celebrations. It was something I could use to bring attention to his name. The other elements I wanted to capture were his boots and his hat, specifically a hat with the Virgen de Guadalupe. He worked in construction, and the altar displays his boots and hat. The foundation of the altar is 'built' of concepts that I felt were close to him, based on the family's description. I represented his heritage though the colors on the *papel picado* and the yo-yo garland, which are from the Mexican flag. In

several photos, he had clothing with 'Mexico' or the eagle from the Mexican flag. For his love of singing, I used a background fabric with musical notes.

"There were two things that struck me and connected me to Valente. One, he was shot and killed in my community. Two, his death occurred in the context of a welfare check, a request made by his daughter because she was worried. As a behavioral health nurse, I have received those kinds of calls from family members who are concerned or scared by the behaviors of their loved ones. I've called the local police department to check on patients or have been a part of the decision for a certificate of evaluation to be issued to bring a patient into the hospital. The worry is always present that having the police show up at a patient's door can potentially escalate the situation, leading to the patient getting harmed or killed."

■ MICHELLE VALENCIA-STARK, MAKER

## Bevin Todd Chippewa's Life Was Stolen in Blackfoot, Idaho, in 2019

"I felt fortunate to be able to stitch for Bevin Todd Chippewa. I have had an affection since childhood for the eastern front of northern Montana, the land of his birth. I was only able to find a small bit of public information about him and long to know more. I read a lot into the few photographic images I discovered online. **He had such a kind face and appeared to be part of a loving family.**

"Public records suggest he suffered a good deal in his short life. The circumstances of his death may argue that the availability of weapons in times of emotional distress can be fatal. I told myself a lot of stories about his life as I stitched, embroidering connections between us. The vintage quilt squares were pieced by hand by anonymous women in times past. I included them because my favorite photo of Bevin with what may have been family members had a quilt on the wall. Quilts can powerfully unite us." ■ HEIKI READ, MAKER

## Gabriel Fernandez's Life Was Stolen in Palmdale, California, in 2013

"Gabriel Fernandez was an eight-year-old boy who died in May 2013 after being severely abused and tortured by his mother and her boyfriend, both of whom were arrested and convicted for his death.

"The halftone pattern in his portrait represents the media frenzy that followed his tortured death. **The flowers are in memory of the beautiful boy he was.** The text on the quilt block framing his portrait reads: 'Beaten, starved, shot by his mother & boyfriend. Caught in our systems that couldn't care enough.'

"*Note:* In 2020, Netflix premiered a six-part documentary telling the tragic life story of this boy. The documentary is titled *The Trials of Gabriel Fernandez*." ■ ANONYMOUS, MAKER

## Keyla Salazar's Life Was Stolen
## in Gilroy, California, in 2019

"Keyla Salazar was described by many as 'Sunshine.' In the words of her family and friends, she was strong, smart, beautiful, vibrant, and pure. She was one of three victims killed when a nineteen-year-old gunman opened fire with an AK-47 assault rifle purchased legally in Nevada in the weeks prior to the Gilroy Garlic Festival, attended by 100,000 people, in Gilroy, California. Sixteen others were wounded before the gunman turned the gun on himself. Law enforcement could not determine the shooter's motivation, although his social media reflected his contacts with white-supremacist ideology.

"Keyla was a bright young thirteen-year-old, who would've celebrated her fourteenth birthday one week from the shooting. Her family said she spent the morning of the shooting completing chores to convince her parents to buy her a puppy. As I worked on this remembrance banner and looked so many times into Keyla's eyes and sweet face, I was moved by her tragic story. I too live on the central coast of California, and I remember the shock and sadness we all felt as we heard of the mass shooting at the Gilroy Garlic Festival.

**"Gun violence is a national epidemic.** There has never been a more urgent time for lawmakers to pass commonsense legislation that limits the availability of assault-style weapons, to prevent tragedies such as this and far too many others." ■ RUTH SMITH, MAKER

# Victor McElhaney's Life Was Stolen
# in Los Angeles, California, in 2019

"Victor McElhaney, a talented 21-year-old music student at the University of Southern California, Thornton, was shot and killed on March 10, 2019. Victor was with friends several blocks from campus when approached by either three or four men, who attempted to rob them. Victor was shot and died later that day.

"Victor's parents say that he was drumming before he could walk or talk. He played music growing up and studied at the East Bay Center for Performing Arts. At USC, he was part of the jazz studies program and was interested in the relationship between music and social and political movements. He also mentored young musicians and taught at the Oakland Public Conservatory of Music. He was an active member of USC's Center for Black Cultural and Student Affairs. **Victor believed in the healing power of music and hoped to use the power of music as a tool for social activism.**

"As I learned about Victor, I was struck by his wide circle of friends and the wonderful remembrances they had. He clearly was a young man who was not only loved but had already made a difference in the world—and had so much more to give. His death is an enormous loss. More than 700 family members, friends, and fellow musicians gathered on the USC campus for a celebration of Victor's life. An endowed scholarship in Victor's name is a part of his legacy.

"I chose to use the USC colors, red and gold, for the block. In addition to the loss of Victor in 2019, his family also lost Torian Hughes, a child they helped raise and considered one of their own, to gun violence in 2017. Torian's killer was on trial when Victor was murdered. Such loss is hard to fathom. I hope I captured Victor's beautiful smile in my block. His story touched me deeply, and I feel honored to be a part of this project." ■ MARCIA MERSKY, MAKER

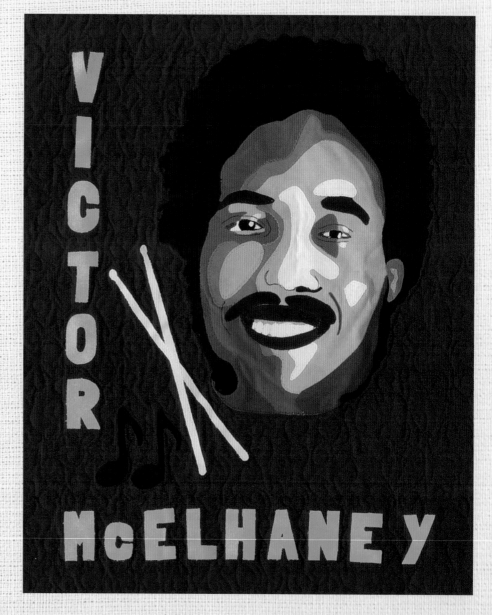

## Tommy Le's Life Was Stolen
### in Seattle, Washington, in 2018

"It has been an honor to participate in the Social Justice Sewing Academy Remembrance Project. I put my appliqué and embroidery skills to the test on this block honoring the life of Tommy Le.

"Tommy was described as a 'bubbly kid.' Looking at the few photos of him available online, his smile is infectious, so I wanted to try to capture that in my portrait. He used to garden with his grandmother, so I used petals as the background. He was from Burien, Washington, and was the child of Vietnamese immigrants who had come to the U.S. to escape police violence. **He loved playing chess, reading, and eating Flamin' Hot Cheetos.** He had talked of becoming a firefighter and had plans to attend a local community college.

"In June 2017, responding to a 911 call about a man possibly armed with a knife, a King County deputy shot Tommy three times, once in the hand and twice in the back. Police exhaustively searched for a knife but found only a pen. Tommy Le died a few hours before he would have graduated from high school. A pen is not a knife. But even if they had found a knife, that is no justification for Tommy Le's extrajudicial killing." ■ **MADDIE ROMANSIC, MAKER**

# Jordan Baker's Life Was Stolen
## in Houston, Texas, in 2014

"In 2014, Jordan Baker was killed for riding his bike while Black. There was no legitimate motive for his senseless murder. He was a young man, just 26 years old, a father and a son who lived in Houston, Texas. Jordan was unarmed while riding his bike through a shopping center when he was approached by an off-duty police officer who was working as a security guard. A few minutes later, Jordan was shot dead. A grand jury reviewed evidence and security footage and found no evidence that Jordan had done anything suspicious. **However, the officer was never disciplined and remains on the force.**

"The location where Jordan was shot is just a few miles from where I live, so I drove there to see the shopping center. As I made this block, I tried to think of the happy days he surely had in his short life, and I tried not to focus on his worst day. I found a photo of him smiling, and that is how I wanted to depict him. I was honored to be asked to make this small work of art in his memory." ■ TERESA DURYEA WONG, MAKER

MARLEN OCHOA-LOPEZ

## Marlen Ochoa-Lopez's Life Was Stolen
## in Chicago, Illinois, in 2019

"In April of 2019, Marlen Ochoa-Lopez was brutally murdered. She was nineteen years old, married, mother of a three-year-old son, and nine months pregnant with her second child. Marlen responded to a Craigslist post by a woman who said she was selling baby clothes and a stroller. Once there, her killers strangled her, cut her baby from her womb, and placed her body in a garbage can in the backyard. Because of the way the baby was taken from her womb, the child suffered brain damage. After the attack, the woman who murdered Marlen called 911 saying she had just given birth to a child. Once examined at the hospital, the woman showed no signs of having given birth, yet the hospital failed to notify the police or government child services. The newborn was put on life support. It wasn't until after Marlen's body was found that it was determined through DNA testing that the baby in the hospital was Marlen's. The family is pushing for a bill referred to as 'Marlen's Law' to check the identities of newborns brought into a hospital.

"My son and I worked together to create this piece in memory of Marlen. I asked him to paint a portrait of Marlen knowing that would be the focus of the block. I chose to surround her portrait with a baby quilt, representing love and warmth. The fabric selections include fabric with houses on it, fabrics used in other baby quilts, and a final border with hearts on it as a way of connecting Marlen to her children and family, which meant so much to her. Marlen is remembered by family and friends as a sweet, respectful person. **She was deeply loved by her mother, father, husband, son, and many more.** I remember reading about the details of Marlen's death in Chicago in 2019 and thinking, how do you go on, knowing that your child died such a horrific death? The pain must be unbearable."

■ PAULA ZAJAC AND HARLAN BALLOGG, MAKERS

# More Stolen Lives

Quilted remembrance banners are also shown for the following stolen lives.

**See these banners on page 110:**

**Etonne Tanzymore** … in Baltimore, Maryland, in 2020;
Maker: Julie Vician

**Walter Scott** … in North Charleston, South Carolina,
in 2015; Maker: Camela Guevara

**Jeremy Sanchez** … in El Monte, California, in 2018;
Maker: Vicki Keller

**Gina Montalto** … in Parkland, Florida, in 2018;
Maker: Elisabeth Geller

**See these banners on page 111:**

**Yahira Nesby** … in Brooklyn, New York, in 2019;
Maker: Elizabeth Wong

**Aracely Hoffman** … in Hilo, Hawaii, in 2016;
Maker: Becky Kronstad

**Aiyana Mo'Nay Stanley-Jones** … in Detroit, Michigan,
in 2010; Maker: Alissa Haight Carlton

**Jordan Edwards** … in Balch Springs, Texas, in 2017;
Maker: Cheryl Lawrence

**See these banners on page 112:**

**Jason Pero** … Bad River Indian Reservation, Wisconsin,
in 2018; Maker: Sonya Walton

**Tatiana Hall** … in Philadelphia, Pennsylvania, in 2020;
Maker: Gabby Coburn

**Steven Alire Jr.** … in Grand Junction, Colorado,
in 2020; Maker: Stephanie Z. Ruyle

**Junior Prosper** … in Miami, Florida, in 2015;
Maker: Nancy Overton

**See these banners on page 113:**

**Akai Gurley** … in Brooklyn, New York, in 2014;
Maker: Sylvia Hernandez

**Botham Jean** … in Dallas, Texas, in 2018;
Maker: Alicia Marcha

**Brian Quinones** … in Edina, Minnesota, in 2019;
Maker: Anonymous

**Shai'India Harris** … in Portland, Oregon, in 2020;
Maker: Chris Batten

**See these banners on page 114:**

**Natalia Wallace** … in Chicago, Illinois, in 2020;
Maker: Didi Skidmore

**Juston Root** … in Brookline, Massachusetts, in 2020;
Maker: Anonymous

**Steven Eugene Washington** … in Los Angeles, California,
in 2010; Maker: Jasmin Hartnell

**Eric Garner** … in Staten Island, New York, in 2014;
Maker: Kelly Martineau

**See these banners on page 115:**

**Michael Ramos** … in Austin, Texas, in 2020;
Maker: Rhonda Anderson

**Jamal Williams** … in Chicago, Illinois, in 2020;
Maker: Dr. Tony Jean Dickerson

**Shukri Ali Said** … in Atlanta, Georgia, in 2018;
Maker: Heather Schulte

**Charles Parker** … in Athens, Georgia, in 2012;
Maker: Amy Trueman

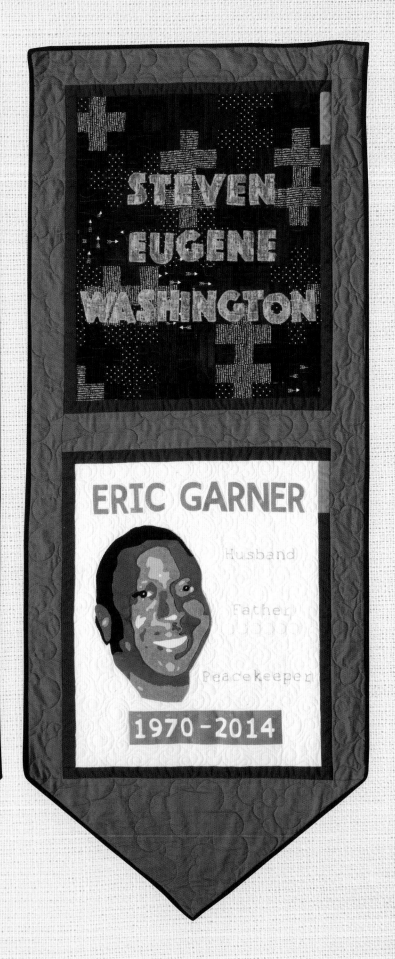

NATALIA WALLACE · 7 YEARS OLD
JULY 4, 2020

SWEET CREATIVE
JOYFUL DREAMER
BRIGHT CURIOUS
RADIANT SMART
PLAYFUL HAPPY
PRECIOUS HEART
INNOCENT SASSY
VIBRANT
ARTISTIC
LOVING
BEAUTIFUL
SHY

JUSTON
✝
ROOT

STEVEN
EUGENE
WASHINGTON

ERIC GARNER

Husband

Father

Peacekeeper

1970–2014

## One Quilter's Studio Space Emerges as the Heart and Soul of SJSA: Nancy Williams

■ The Social Justice Sewing Academy (SJSA) does not have an office. There is no fancy headquarters building with paid staff. This organization is 100 percent grassroots with volunteers spread all over the United States, Canada, and other locales. **But if there were one dwelling where the heart and soul of SJSA existed, it would be Nancy Williams's sewing studio.**

In the start-up days of SJSA, just about every quilt, every block, and every piece of textile art passed through the doors of Nancy's second-floor Oakland, California, workroom. When she and her husband became empty nesters, they downsized their home considerably. So Nancy decided to branch out and rented space on the second story of a mixed-use commercial building to house her quilt-sewing equipment, fabric stash, thread collection, and various other tools and notions needed to make quilts. Like hundreds of thousands of quilters around the world, Nancy finishes three-layer quilts using a longarm machine. A longarm machine is a large sewing machine mounted on rails, typically twelve to fifteen feet long, which can easily slide back and forth over a quilt while stitching. These machines consume a lot of square footage, and with her rented space, Nancy's beloved studio is bigger than her entire home. **Inside this industrial room, Nancy has devoted countless hours to putting the finishing touches on so many SJSA community quilts, blocks, and banners that she has lost count.**

Nancy got involved with SJSA in its early days, when she answered a call for volunteer longarm quilters. Social justice issues were always important to her, and she has been an advocate for most of her life. So when she learned about the mission of SJSA, it was a perfect avenue to combine her advocacy with her skills in quilting, her equipment, and eventually even her studio space to help nurture this young organization.

Nancy describes the SJSA concept as brilliant. **She finds the SJSA methodology of giving young people the opportunity to express themselves with fabric art, and ultimately helping them realize they have voices, a powerful opportunity that is bound to have a positive, lasting effect on the makers.** The next step, of involving countless adult volunteers in the process, is equally important and is a powerful tool to build empathy among a large pool of volunteer sewists, embroiderers, and quilters.

With her skill set as an accomplished quilter and her determination to spend her time on something that will bring lasting change, Nancy is carefully finishing textile blocks into stunning art quilts and banners. In turn, these community-crafted quilts are forever capturing youth voices and recording them as permanent, quilted art. Thanks to her time, talent, and establishing her studio as the heart and soul of SJSA, Nancy is helping present and forever preserve the most overlooked voices in our communities.

Nancy Williams has dedicated countless hours, supporting SJSA, and she has completed community quilts, individual quilts, and banners on her longarm quilting machine.

# A Massachusetts High School Student Learns to Lead: Bianca Mercado

■ One student at a high school in Cambridge, Massachusetts, hosted a workshop on colorism to help other students feel comfortable in their own skin color. That same student produced a film about the importance of names and how kids of color sometimes butcher their own names to make them easier for White people to pronounce. She was invited to join an activist group no one aspires to join, Sisters Unchained, a nonprofit for women and girls with an incarcerated parent. And when large swaths of her high school student body decided to form a walkout to honor the Black Lives Matter movement, she was among them. **That young woman, Bianca Mercado, possesses an outsize portion of courage.**

Bianca has spent countless hours of her young life advocating for serious community issues. She has dreams of attending college and obtaining a postgraduate degree in social work. One of the most important tools in her activist kit is art. She identifies herself as an artist who loves watercolor. She also self-identifies as Latinx, a queer woman, and a student, who lives with her dad and a dog.

**As the Social Justice Sewing Academy expanded across the United States, Bianca was a natural choice to take a leadership role in facilitating workshops for students.** In those workshops, Bianca used fabric, glue, scissors, and sewing machines to do what she always does—help others discover their voice and find the courage to express the concerns and problems that impact their everyday life. She is a perfect example of an individual with leadership skills who can step in and help SJSA do its thing. During the time she facilitated workshops, Bianca was essentially a kid teaching kids. But it was her courage, her maturity, and her skills as an artist and activist that enabled the students to learn from a fellow student.

The first SJSA youth movement workshops she facilitated started in her own community, Boston, and then she began traveling as a facilitator to host sessions across the country. While she was teaching other kids, she was also learning. She discovered that some of her West Coast kids had a lot of environmental concerns, while other parts of the country focused on violence and gun control. One workshop included a group of girls with family members that were incarcerated.

**The things Bianca learned inspired both her art and her activism.** She spent an entire summer making a large art quilt that employed every letter of the alphabet to raise awareness for a critical social justice issue, a problem in society, or a leader who's made a difference. For example, F is for Flint (Michigan), H is for Holocaust, and S is for School to Prison Pipeline. Now, as this quilt is exhibited and shared on social media, Bianca feels a sense of pride in the quilt as a work of activist art, and she also is proud of the technical skills she mastered to make appliquéd fabric pieces behave like paint. Once she constructed the layout, embroidery volunteers secured the appliqué to the background, and then the long banners were beautifully machine quilted by Nancy Williams.

With funding from an SJSA grant, in 2016 Bianca traveled to Cuba to study, learn, see, and absorb this Latino culture with its long and complicated history. While she contemplated the remnants of Communism and studied the rich colors in Cuban art, she also wanted to bring home something of this culture and its people. But rather than shop at tourist traps or typical retail shops, Bianca scoured thrift stores and purchased secondhand clothing and textiles. She brought these treasures back to her home and set to work on a series of art quilts and panels that she refers to as her "Cuba mosaics." The text is in Spanish and the subject matter reflects the colors and culture she absorbed during her visit. One quilt is dedicated to "Comunismo" and another is a negative-space appliqué portrait featuring "Che," the revolutionary hero Ernesto "Che" Guevara. Bianca's Cuba series and the quilted alphabet banners are an integral part of the SJSA portfolio. They are tactile examples of the power of social justice outreach on the student, the viewer, and even the maker.

**CHE** 43″ × 43″ | UPCYCLED FABRIC FROM CUBA
RAW-EDGE APPLIQUÉ BY BIANCA MERCADO
HAND EMBROIDERY BY A VOLUNTEER
MACHINE QUILTED BY NANCY WILLIAMS

**COMUNISMO**
UPCYCLED FABRIC FROM CUBA
BY BIANCA MERCADO
MACHINE QUILTED BY NANCY WILLIAMS

**ACTIVIST ABCs**  SIX PANELS, COTTON | APPLIQUÉ BY BIANCA MERCADO
HAND EMBROIDERY BY SJSA VOLUNTEERS | MACHINE QUILTED BY NANCY WILLIAMS | 2019

**TOP:** The quilt was awarded first place at the Modern Quilt Guild QuiltCon juried competition in 2019 in the youth category.

**LEFT:** Detail block—W's for White Supremacy—of *Activist ABCs* (see full panels, above)

# Veteran Youth Leader Learns While Teaching: Amin Robinson

■ At the tender age of 21, Amin Robinson has accomplished more than most people twice his age. He is an energetic young man with a passion so intense you can see it in his gentle smile. Here is just a short list of the jobs, volunteer roles, and leadership gigs in his impressive resume: mental health coach for trauma victims; volunteer tutor in English language and literacy skills for Hispanic elementary students; after-school staff providing a safe place for children with working parents; driver's education tutor; leader of a club for anime enthusiasts; grocery store worker; budding author of anime graphic novels featuring Black characters; cosplay costume designer; and prekindergarten teacher in the Oakland, California, public schools.

During all of this, Amin found his way to the Social Justice Sewing Academy, not as a student but as a workshop facilitator. He was attracted to the organization because he feels it offers a critical opportunity, and a safe space, for young people to talk about the issues that are important to them. Amin has experienced enough in his young life to know that most teenagers and young adults do not have the opportunity, encouragement, or frankly even the time, to stop and think about the injustices they face and how to fix them. **He wants to foster those conversations and empower youth to think differently and recognize that they can take an active role in trying to make their life better.**

He just never imagined that a sewing machine would be part of that activism. Before SJSA entered his life, Amin had never done much more than attempt to mend his jeans. Now he is interested in learning to sew and plans to purchase a sewing machine in the near future. In addition to sewing art for social justice, he is also interested in designing his own line of cosplay costumes and sewing them himself.

While facilitating SJSA workshops, Amin was of course juggling his paid jobs and other leadership activities. He did not have a car, and he often walked or took public transportation. Once he started volunteering with SJSA, though, he expanded his network of other SJSA leaders and they all supported one another, even driving to pick him up on occasion. While these young leaders were together, Amin feels he learned much more than he taught. He started thinking much more creatively, and fully endorsed the entrepreneurial spirit of SJSA and its community. It was eye-opening to see how the organization started small and has grown to involve so many people from so many walks of life.

For Amin, the experience of enticing students of color to talk about social justice issues is extremely rewarding. Each of them has lived a different reality, and almost all of them have suffered injustice in one form or another. They are well aware of the issues, they just don't have the skills to express those injustices or recognize how to take action. Amin takes pride in knowing he is helping raise those voices. And that's why he invests something that is most precious to him—*time*—in this organization and its community.

# Building the Educational Model: Suzanne Schmidt

■ Suzanne Schmidt possesses the perfect profile to help support the education component of SJSA. She is patient, calm, and credible. Suzanne holds a PhD in English and is an activist in her community, and on top of that, she enjoys sewing.

She is thrilled to see the hundreds of adult SJSA volunteers move from awareness to action as they sew, embroider, and quilt blocks and textile art made by others. **As they hold these textile stories in their hands, Suzanne knows each individual is holding someone's voice, their frustrations, even their dreams for a better future, and that these connections are powerful and lasting.**

Suzanne has authored academic articles on the power of craft as a way to express dissent. She is acutely aware that the concept of liberty and justice for all is actually not applied equally across America. And when she hears people in the community who disagree with this concept, she tries to help them reflect about where those feelings are coming from and offer ways in which they could build empathy. Suzanne believes craft is one answer.

She has hosted numerous SJSA youth movement workshops for youth in California, and she is always moved to learn their stories. While launching discussions on social justice, Suzanne carefully guides students as they navigate sensitive issues, and she keeps them talking about the possibility of change. For Suzanne, the most potent way to use craft as activism is to focus on the twin idea of critique and advocacy for change. **By pointing teenagers toward activism and recognizing things they can change, rather than just observing, this volunteer draws on her strong academic experience to help define and elevate the voice of these young people.**

# An All-Around Awesome Volunteer: Cedric Tanner

■ When SJSA calls, Cedric Tanner is the first to answer. He has volunteered since the founding of SJSA and his list of tasks is just about anything Sara Trail asks him to do. He first met SJSA founder Sara Trail at a time when he was seeking to get his professional life in order, and Sara's mentorship was a lifesaver for Cedric. Now he is willing to help her with "all that sewing stuff" whenever duty calls.

Cedric works at several jobs, and some of his work was turned upside down during the Covid pandemic. For example, he was a home health care worker, but his clients were uncomfortable bringing people into their home while quarantining. Cedric also works for Amazon and is an employee of a drug and alcohol addiction center, Archway Recovery Services, in Solano County, California. This recovery center turned out to be a perfect place to host a workshop on social justice and introduce the SJSA mission.

Many of the people who seek treatment at the center are transitioning from prison back into society, and they have firsthand experience with systemic racism and myriad social injustices. Cedric believes in these individuals, most of whom are men, and he treats each one of them with respect. He knows all too well that many of them had difficult childhoods or other stressful life situations.

If the men whom Cedric mentors have been incarcerated, Cedric never asks them what crime they committed, or about their past lives. He doesn't want that picture of them in his mind. **Rather, he wants to help them find their way to a better life, a life that is peaceful, productive, and free from addiction.**

Cedric's role at the treatment center expands beyond that of just a paid employee. He also wears his SJSA volunteer hat proudly and looks for opportunities to expand the organization's work in his community. So it was a natural fit that he would volunteer to lead an SJSA workshop at Archway Recovery Services. The sessions began with a serious, and lengthy, group discussion about social justice and what it really means. Each adult had a strong sense of the different definitions of social justice and shared what it means to them personally. Next, they were challenged to figure out how to translate their message into cloth. Cedric explained that they would each be making a textile art block, which would later be sewn into a large quilt. While very few of them had experience with fabric or appliqué, many of them are seasoned artists, having honed their craft while they were incarcerated.

Through the SJSA workshop, these men are given the opportunity to express what is important to them and the confirmation that viewers will take note when these quilts are displayed publicly. The men were proud to learn that their blocks would travel around the country and serve as a vital reminder that each of us has a voice and each of us deserves to be heard.

# A Dynamic Young Advocate and Future Leader: Jocelyn Gama Garcia

■ Social justice and equality are just some of the issues that inspire Jocelyn Gama to spend countless hours of her young life as an activist and advocate. Between classes at the University of California, Berkeley, and her job, she somehow finds time to volunteer to advocate for tenants in public housing and mentor middle school kids. Needless to say, Jocelyn is an accomplished young woman with big plans for the future.

With all this on her plate, she still finds the energy and enthusiasm to volunteer for SJSA. She taught her first youth workshop in the summer of 2019—a six-week course. Jocelyn even helped design the format and message for that workshop while working closely with Sara Trail.

**Jocelyn is a firm believer in grabbing every opportunity that comes her way, if it means there is a chance she can bring about real change.** She is deeply committed to righting many of the wrongs that people of color face in society.

Jocelyn is a volunteer advocate for the East Bay Housing Organizations, a nonprofit that works to ensure low-income families have access to affordable housing, a particularly critical problem for the Bay Area of California. Advocates like Jocelyn help educate community leaders and businesses about the problems and promote solutions to help alleviate the crisis. For many families in the area, access to affordable housing is a constant battle that takes a toll on young children when they are constantly uprooted. Ultimately, housing, or the lack thereof, can be one of the most critical factors in a system filled with systemic racism. A new generation of bright and engaged young adults like Jocelyn are hoping to crack open those problems and make progress in the fight for equality.

When Jocelyn stood up to lead her first youth workshop for SJSA, she didn't have much experience in sewing or quiltmaking. But what she did have was strong leadership skills and intense passion, uncommon qualities in someone just nineteen years old at the time. Interestingly, although some of her family members work in the garment and sewing industry, Jocelyn has made only a few attempts to sew. Instead, she found a better use for her skills—leading others.

She especially loves the beginning of a workshop like the one she taught for six weeks, where everyone starts to talk about social justice and what it means to them. Jocelyn says the maturity that these young people bring to the forefront when talking about the issues they face as people of color are just amazing to hear. She likes to steer the conversation to power. Jocelyn challenges her students to consider power—who has it and what do they do with it? From there, she begins to offer counsel on how to change that narrative, and therein lies the crux of social justice. **When marginalized communities and unheard voices begin to think about their own power and how to use it to steer the narrative, the opportunity for meaningful change opens up.**

In addition to teaching teenagers through SJSA, Jocelyn has also mentored middle school students. Again, she found the conversation these kids of color had amazing. When talking about social justice issues, even students as young as sixth grade were well aware of the legal stance, and unfortunately the implications, of redlining (a series of discriminatory practices by federal and local governments to deny services or raise prices in certain communities). These kids live the fallout of redlining, and it is particularly prevalent in dense, urban communities like the Bay Area. One can only imagine how devastating it must have been for these young students when then President Trump stood on a podium in front of throngs of people and stated that Oakland, California, their home—a place where they struggled for their slice of the American pie—was "hell."

In February 2020, Jocelyn found yet another opportunity to teach, but this time it was adults. She led two

workshops at QuiltCon in Austin, Texas. QuiltCon is a large sewing and quilting convention sponsored by the Modern Quilt Guild. In this case, her students were highly skilled quiltmakers, but what they learned from Jocelyn and the SJSA message helped them see a path to combine quilting with activism. **While creating quilt blocks from cotton, they created fabric art that emphasized social justice messages geared to erase inequality and build empathy for people of all colors and walks of life.** And surely, learning how to do this from an instructor as young and power-ful as Jocelyn helped solidify the message.

In addition to teaching, Jocelyn also stood for hours at the SJSA quilt exhibit at QuiltCon answering questions and engaging with viewers about the unusual and, for many, unexpected messages sewn into the community quilts on view.

Finally, she found the time to make a quilt of her own. Quilting is not something she has a lot of free time for right now, but that's okay. Jocelyn is making enormous progress in the quilting community, and of course beyond, by using her super skills as a leader, advocate, and bright young voice fighting for social justice.

■ Sara Trail and Lauren Black are a perfect duo to run a community organization. While Sara talks fast and thinks far ahead, Lauren speaks slowly and is patient, poised, and incredibly focused. In her role as the executive director, Lauren's skill set will help build SJSA for the future.

The two first met during college and remained close friends. At first, Lauren was Sara's sounding board, helping her make new ideas become a reality. **But when Lauren was asked to lead the organization in December 2020, she quickly demonstrated her leadership skills and her ability to meticulously manage not only the back-end business systems, but also a rapidly growing list of volunteers and multiple programs.**

Lauren was born and raised in the Los Angeles area. After high school, she moved to Vermont to attend college. The sudden move from a diverse, urban city to a rural, and mostly White, community was a shock to the young college freshman. However, as time went on, her experiences there helped guide her to the decision to pursue a master's degree in educational psychology from Loyola Marymount University. For her day job, Lauren works as an educational psychologist in schools that support minority populations. Her role as the executive director of SJSA is unpaid.

Lauren has big dreams for SJSA. Her vision is multi-tiered. First, build the business, accounting, and financial systems to keep the organization on strong footing. These are thankless tasks, carried out behind the scenes, yet they are critical to every organization. Next, grow the outreach and expand SJSA's capabilities.

On a personal note, Lauren is frustrated that it took the death of George Floyd to wake up the country. Yet she is simultaneously grateful that so many people are now focused on the issues of systemic racism and social injustice. She is encouraged by the huge influx of SJSA volunteers who have stepped up to support the organization, and she feels incredibly hopeful when she sees the hundreds of beautiful works of art contributed by volunteers.

While makers reflect on the lives that have been stolen, Lauren is also seeing the makers themselves become enlightened, and that is the most rewarding part of leading SJSA. Lauren has been personally connected to some of the families who have received Memory Quilts, and she understands their struggles. She and other SJSA volunteers realize that regardless of the flaws of the individual whose life was stolen, they were part of a family and they had friends and family who loved them. As those families mourn, Lauren hopes the quilts they are gifted bring a sense of comfort. **Her goal is to continue supporting this effort by connecting motivated and talented volunteers who are capable of making beautiful, handmade quilted works to as many families as possible.** In addition, she appreciates the enormous potential of the Remembrance Project's quilted banners, honoring victims of violent crimes, to influence viewers around the country.

Going forward, Lauren ultimately hopes the SJSA message is heard and remembered. There are so many things that need to change in our society to end racism and right the wrongs, and Lauren knows these things will take time. But every step forward counts, and as the leader of this young yet strong community organization, Lauren will help carry SJSA forward and ensure it remains directed toward making a difference.

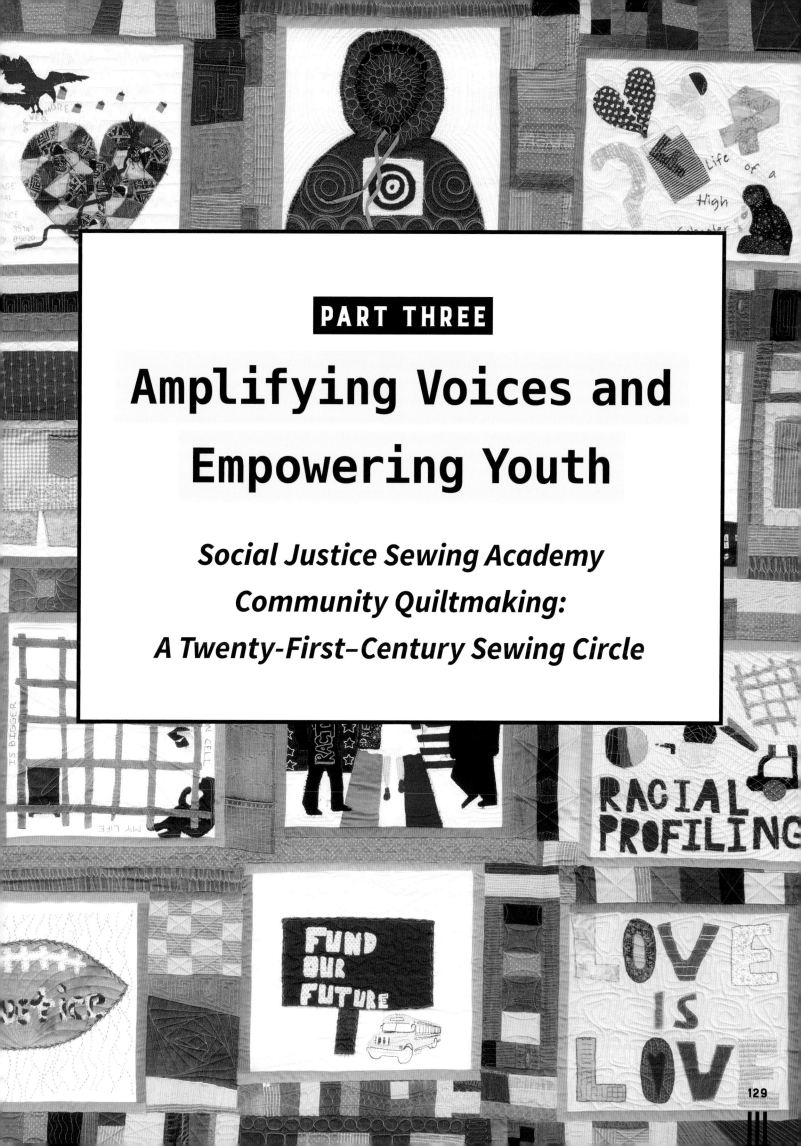

# PART THREE

# Amplifying Voices and Empowering Youth

*Social Justice Sewing Academy*
*Community Quiltmaking:*
*A Twenty-First–Century Sewing Circle*

## THE WORLD IS A NOISY PLACE. WE ARE CONSTANTLY BOMBARDED BY WORDS AND IMAGES.

Violence happens, and it is blasted across our screens, over and over. Beauty happens too, and humans gravitate toward that beauty. Amid all this, we clamor to communicate with one another. Communicating connects one human to another. Communicating releases our emotions.

Often, it can be difficult to be heard above the noise. It can be a struggle to release your feelings in a way that others can hear, remember, or respond to. For Black, Indigenous, and people of color, making your voice heard is especially problematic, and righting this wrong is one of the founding pillars of the Social Justice Sewing Academy. SJSA is uniquely focused on creating opportunities for expression in a way that allows the makers to speak, to release their emotions, and to communicate with a myriad of people whom they would otherwise never reach.

Through the creation of textile art, these voices are forever preserved with needle and thread. These messages of injustice, violence, racism, wealth disparity, gentrification, environmental issues, poverty, and even beauty are sewn into these quilted works of art. These voices are amplified. They are rising above the noise. And the process is helping empower these makers.

"There's really no such thing as the 'voiceless.' There are only the deliberately silenced, or the preferably unheard."

■ ARUNDHATI ROY, AUTHOR

## Stephanie Valencia: The Making of the SJSA *Critical Race Theory* Community Quilt

The first task Stephanie Valencia tackled in her 2019 workshop for at-risk high school students was to help the students unlearn. Once the group of twenty teenagers began talking about their lives and the challenges of people of color, she quickly realized they knew very little about social justice, and what they did know had been presented to them through the lens of White privilege. As they began breaking down the concept, the discussion flowed to specific historical events and, most important, the repercussions of those incidents for students of color and their families today.

The theme of reparations was an obvious choice. Many people assume that *reparations* simply means a monetary award. But the broader concept is infinitely more complex. **Reparations actually involve methods for how to erase the systemic injustices still in existence today, primarily by changing the way we think, shifting our fundamental philosophy, and transforming our justice system.**

Stephanie is not a professional teacher, a quilter, or a textile artist. She volunteered to host this workshop after seeing an exhibition of SJSA community quilts in Ogden, Utah, where she was living at the time. She admits she was a bit nervous before her first day of the six-week workshop, which was held at an alternative high school in Ogden. But once she got started, she was completely enthralled by the experience. When the students talked about the distinction between what they knew to be true from their own lives and what they had been taught, the ideas began flowing. Everyone agreed to make twenty blocks centered on American history with a critical eye to the Black experience, and they made the quilt a timeline of historical events.

Stephanie helped each student solidify his or her idea and ensure that the concept was transferable to fabric. For some of the young people, this was the toughest part because some ideas are too esoteric to be communicated in one simple textile block. **But ultimately, twenty events were chosen, and by cutting up fabric and making art, the students found a way to express themselves. They found their voices.**

They had oodles of fabric to choose from thanks to generous donors from around the United States, who shipped boxes of fabric to Stephanie's doorstep. And when a student needed a piece of fabric with a special color or design, Stephanie went to a local quilt retail shop and purchased it. While the teenagers worked on their art during the six-week course, the atmosphere was bright and fun. But things changed on the last day, when the students were asked to write artist statements about their blocks and what they meant to them. Stephanie witnessed these kids tackle the assignment with a seriousness she had not seen before. The atmosphere was somber, and everyone worked hard. When it was time to share their statements, these teenagers showed maturity beyond their years as they supported one another and shared their own personal hardships. For Stephanie, being in the room to hear these stories was a heart-wrenching and unforgettable experience.

The SJSA *Critical Race Theory* community quilt is a raw expression of the horrors and tragedies of American history that is typically not part of standard curriculum. As viewers have the chance to see this quilt in person, they too will certainly walk away with a greater empathy for parts of our history and its lasting repercussions today. And one day this quilt, along with the other activist undertakings of our times, will help bring about a meaningful understanding of the true definition of *reparations*.

**CRITICAL RACE THEORY COMMUNITY QUILT**
MADE BY HIGH SCHOOL STUDENTS IN OGDEN, UTAH
PIECED BY SARA TRAIL | MACHINE QUILTED BY NANCY WILLIAMS | 2019

The strip-pieced designs running through this quilt represent the number of people who made the difficult journey to freedom.

### ROW 1, BLOCK 1: AFRICA BY MELINA Z.

"Too often, images of savagery, poverty, and deviance are used to justify gross human-rights violations. Participants in the transatlantic slave trade used these images to create a culture of dominance and oppression, believing themselves to be the saviors of a group of people incapable of governing their own lives. Africans were labeled as primitive and barbaric—a people in need of the structure that White masters and slavery provided them.

"This scene displays three tribes of women and two children at the water's edge, living the last free day of their lives. Colorful batik fabrics symbolize the vibrancy that these individuals had before being stripped of their tribal robes and jewelry and being cast into chains and rags. The women's demeanor is regal as they preside over playful children while gathering food and water for their families. This block shows the beauty of the African people before slavery and colonialism destroyed their lives and civilizations. It is meant to destroy the image of superiority that many individuals project onto something or someone that doesn't conform to White Anglo-Saxon standards and ideology."

### ROW 1, BLOCK 2: AUCTION BY ISIS R.

"What is the accumulation of all your successes, loves, and freedoms worth, from birth to death? How does $36,000 USD sound? That is what the average price of an enslaved person in the 1800s translates to today. It was at the auction block that families were torn apart. Slaves would beg the bidders to purchase their children or loved ones along with them. It did not matter. By categorizing and auctioning enslaved persons alongside livestock, the dehumanization of an entire race of people had begun. This block represents the beginning of the horrors and oppression that Black people faced upon arriving in America. The newly enslaved Africans stand larger than life, symbolizing the smallness and lack of morality that the White auctioneer demonstrates. The use of bold batiks in browns and golds shows that these individuals, though stripped of their dignity and sold among beasts, will not forget their royal origins. They carry with them the strength to survive slavery."

### ROW 1, BLOCK 3: BREASTFEEDING BY MARIAH A.

"White colonial society found the practice of breastfeeding to be animalistic and beneath well-to-do White women. Initially, the wealthy employed lower-class White women as wet nurses, but as slavery grew, domestic enslaved persons became the new plantation wet-nurse. Enslaved mothers would be pulled from their newborns to reside in the plantation home and nurse the master's baby. These women attempted to supplement their own baby's nutrition with other forms of milk and dirty water, causing disease and death. The enslaved mother was forced to watch her own children wither and die while her life's milk fed and strengthened the next generation of oppressors.

"A poem by the contemporary writer and poet Hess Love illustrates this experience with eloquent indignation.

*'I wish I dried up … So the missus babies would dry up too.'* "

### ROW 1, BLOCK 4: THERE'S NO FREEDOM FOR ME BY JASON K.

"This block is inspired by Fredric Douglas's speech, 'What to the Slave is the Fourth of July?' Have you ever thought about the first few Fourth of July celebrations? Imagine colonists' joy at being free from the tyranny of a monarch. Imagine their pride as they birthed a new nation and declared themselves free. Where is the Black man? He is having ointment applied to the lash marks on his back. He is resting before picking the master's cotton in the morning. He is in a stable awaiting tomorrow's auction. This block forces the viewer to associate slavery's scars with the hallmark of Fourth of July symbolism, fireworks. The words so many Americans hold dear to their hearts—life, liberty, and the pursuit of happiness—held no meaning for the Black man in America until almost 100 years after the nation's birth."

### ROW 2, BLOCK 1: UNDERGROUND RAILROAD BY JASMINE L.

"A family of runaway enslaved persons attempts to navigate their way north to freedom via the Underground Railroad. The Underground Railroad operated from the late 1700s until the Civil War, when the clandestine effort led by both Black and White abolitionists moved into the open. There were designated shelters and safe houses known as 'stations,' and the escape routes were provided or led by 'conductors.'

"This scene was not typical, as most escaped enslaved persons were male. The road to freedom was unmarked and dangerous for everyone, but it was especially so for women and children, who were rarely allowed off the plantation and traveled at a slower pace. Young children and infants were difficult to keep silent; every noise risked exposing the group to enslaved-person hunters. Most runaway enslaved persons made their way to border states in the North. After the Fugitive Slave Act passed in 1850, empowering kidnappers and enslaved-person hunters, many former enslaved persons continued even farther north. Those who made it to Canada were granted freedom without fear of recapture."

## ROW 2, BLOCK 2: FORTY ACRES AND A MULE BY JANELLE R.

"Following the abolishment of slavery, Black people were given a brief moment of hope for self-determination. This block depicts the first time this man worked the land on his own terms—the first time his yield would feed his family and build his future. But before the newly freed man could harvest his first crop, his American dream, like his freedom before, was stolen by White men in power.

"Union General William T. Sherman issued Special Field Order #15 after he and President Lincoln's Secretary of War, Edwin Stanton, met with Black leaders in Georgia. They asked these men, 'What do you want for

your people after slavery?' The response was land. Sherman's order declared that over 400,000 acres of land seized from the Confederate rebels would be distributed to Black families in allotments not exceeding 40 acres. No White people would be permitted to live in these communities. It was understood that the freed Black man could not prosper under the rule of those who had enslaved them. Special Field Order #15 was issued on January 16, 1865, during the Civil War. This was America's acknowledgment of the horrors it had inflicted. This was an attempt at reparations.

"So, what happened to '40 acres and a mule'? Shortly after assuming the presidency, Andrew Johnson abolished the order, stripping the land away from the newly freed enslaved persons and handing it back to the masters who had committed treason against their country."

## ROW 2, BLOCK 3: PENAL FARMS BY ALMA M.

*"Neither slavery nor involuntary servitude, except as a punishment for a crime … shall exist within the United States …"* —Thirteenth Amendment to the United States Constitution

"At first glance, it appears that this quilt block depicts enslaved persons picking cotton for their masters. But instead of chains, these men wear stripes. Instead of being the property of a plantation, they are now the property of the state. After slavery was abolished and the promise of reparations was broken, the newly freed Black man was left to figure out how to survive in a society that provided him with nothing and despised his existence. It was difficult to secure employment, and wages were not enough to provide for themselves. The South was suffering economically from the effects of the war and lack of labor.

"Legislators began writing a series of laws that targeted Black people. Black men were arrested for vagrancy, not holding a job, and other petty crimes. They were penalized with fines that they could not pay. Instead of being housed in jails, these individuals were leased to penal farms. Penal farms were a form of legal slavery. The conditions were often worse than slavery, as the wardens had no monetary investment in the inmates. Without any financial loss to them, the inmates were expendable and easily replaceable. Once again, the Black man found himself oppressed, in captivity, and picking the master's cotton."

## ROW 2, BLOCK 4: LYNCHING BY BRITTANY T.

*"Men joked loudly at the sight of the bleeding body ... girls giggled as the flies fed on the blood that dripped from the Negro's nose."*

"This sounds like a passage from a horror story, but it's a line from an article in the *Raleigh Newspaper & Observer* about a 1930 lynching.

"Lynching became common practice in the South during the reconstruction era. Emancipated Blacks were blamed for the woes that befell the states in the aftermath of war. Lynchings were used by White southerners to express their anger and contempt for Black people, as well as to assert white supremacy. Black people were accused of insolence and dubious crimes. They would be arrested and sentenced to death. One of the most frequent complaints that ended in a death sentence during that time was looking at, or speaking to, a White woman.

'Five White Men Take Negro Into Woods; Kill Him: Had Been Charged with Associating with White Women' read an Associated Press headline in Shreveport, Louisiana.

"Lynchings were heinous and celebrated. They were done by small mobs and at big town gatherings. Young children attended and were taught to relish in the appalling nature of the act. The bodies of Black men, women, and children were oftentimes set on fire to the cheers of onlookers. Bodies were dismembered and the mobs would carry away pieces as souvenirs to remind them of the event."

## ROW 3, BLOCK 1: KKK BY JAMAL H.

"The Ku Klux Klan has inflicted brutality upon the Black community for 100 years. The Confederate flag, which is symbolic of the South's rebellion and continued racist acts throughout America, is the backdrop of this piece. It conveys a sense of White nationalism for the KKK and other emerging supremacist groups to rekindle violent memories and incite violence. Their primary goal is to establish white supremacy through intimidation and overt violence directed toward the Black community. Their influence rose in the wake of the reconstruction era in the South. These white supremacists felt threatened by the daily lives of Black individuals living among them, as well as the growing power and influence of African Americans in the South and across the nation.

"The Klan is best known for the terror it inflicted on the Black community during the early to mid-1900s. KKK members burned crosses in the yards of Black people and in public spaces to incite fear and to breed hatred in other White people who harbored resentment but were fearful to act upon it. At the height of the Klan's violence, its members led lynchings, dragging Black people, and at times whole families, from their homes to be killed in front of mobs of all ages."

## ROW 3, BLOCK 2: VOTING BY FELICIA A.

"The Fifteenth Amendment of the U.S. Constitution declared that race or previous servitude would not prevent American citizens from voting. Southern states, wary of Black people's voting power, enacted a system to prevent poor people from voting, a poll tax. They were able to enact these laws without violating the Fifteenth Amendment because they did not single people out by race; however, Black people were the target. So-called grandfather laws were enacted to waive the voting fee for poor Whites.

"It was difficult for a Black man to find work in the South after reconstruction. The jobs he could find weren't adequate to support a family. Poll taxes prevented many Black people from exercising one of U.S. citizens' most prized rights, the right to elect representatives and participate in our democracy. This quilt block shows a line of voters—some White, some Black—with ballot in hand, ready to cast their vote. The Black man in front hangs his head as he realizes that no matter how hard he fights for equality, racial justice is impeded by newly created loopholes in the law. Unlike the White man placing a ballot in the box with a handful of cash, the Black man's ballot will be dropped on the ground to rest at the feet of the next Black man in line."

## ROW 3, BLOCK 3: BROWN V. BOARD OF EDUCATION BY AMANDA L.

*"[I]n the field of public education the doctrine of 'separate but equal' has no place. Separate educational facilities are inherently unequal."* —Chief Justice Earl Warren of the U.S. Supreme Court

"This block is a celebration of Black Americans' supposed victory in the battle for academic equality. There are three Black students standing strong, making their way into an integrated schoolhouse as White segregationists spew hatred and protest the idea of Black people existing and being educated among them. There is a Confederate flag on the pole standing as a symbol of racism and resistance. The American flag flies upside down to represent the dysfunction of civil liberties that the 'separate but equal' doctrine facilitated. In the landmark case of *Brown v. Board of Education*, the Supreme Court ruled in 1954 that schools should no longer be segregated. This ruling did not stop schools from practicing segregation. Do you think overcoming educational segregation had leveled the academic playing field for African Americans in the last 66 years?"

## ROW 3, BLOCK 4: WAR ON DRUGS BY JADA L.

"This block shows 'Public Enemy Number One' behind a red bull's-eye. There are two objects: a marijuana leaf and, behind that, a Black man. Which object is the term referring to? Both. They are one and the same, interchangeable targets and enemies. Drug laws have been used to target certain cultures throughout history. In the nineteenth century, Chinese and other Asian immigrants were targeted in raids on opium dens, while other opiates were sold on grocers' shelves. During the height of the U.S. war on drugs in the 1980s and '90s, crack was targeted and punished at a rate of 100:1 compared with cocaine. Crack is cocaine in rock form and used primarily by Black people; cocaine is the powdered form and is used primarily by White people. Under this sentencing structure, those caught with cocaine would need to have 100 times as much as those caught with crack to receive the same sentence. The American public greatly believes that the war on drugs was enacted to protect them from gun-toting thugs and ever-growing threats of violence. In recent years, light has been shed on its ulterior motives."

## ROW 4, BLOCK 1: FIRE HOSE BY CHANEL B.

"To many, the late 1950s through mid-1960s conjure up images of the American dream, the golden era of economic growth and happiness. It is the image of a family of five piled into the car to visit the local diner. It's TV, Marilyn Monroe, and Elvis. Are there Black people in the mental image you created? Chances are there are not. During this so-called golden era that so many Americans still long for, Black people were eliminated from the picture. They were

not allowed to participate in the American dream. Many people think of segregation as a thing of the distant past that has little effect on today's Black communities, economy, or achievement. Barely a generation has passed since the Civil Rights Act of 1964 that made segregation unconstitutional.

"The quilt square shows a city block lined with mom-and-pop shops. A group of White business owners crowd around a police officer to prevent a Black woman and her child from entering their establishments. The hose, officer, and hydrant are the only splashes of color. This highlights the barbarism that segregationists used and draws attention to the legality of these assaults."

## ROW 4, BLOCK 2: FINES BY RENEE G.

"This block's use of the color orange is to represent the stereo typical orange prison jumpsuit. This Black man's arms are covered by fines and tickets, speaking to the fact that his arrest and incarceration are due to status offenses and racially targeted procedures. Where do you live? In a suburb perhaps? What is the demographic of your neighborhood? White? Imagine police officers patrolling your streets, jumping out of their vehicles, throwing you against the house or facedown on the ground, and cuffing you. Then, they reach into your pockets and search you. All this because you and a couple of neighbors were outside having a beer or friendly conversation. Imagine your kids on the playground playing basketball enduring the same treatment because they looked suspicious in baggy gym clothes. Imagine pulling out of your driveway and being stopped because your car looks too nice for you to own or you don't look like you live in this neighborhood. There would be outrage. That is what it is like to be Black in America."

## ROW 4, BLOCK 3: PRISON INDUSTRIAL COMPLEX BY VANESSA V.

"How much do you think America's leading private prison organization made in 2018? … *48.1 billion dollars*! Private prisons are modern-day penal farms. The privatization of the penal industry came after the implementation of tough-on-crime policies. The state needed more places to warehouse inmates. Private corporations stepped forward and claimed to be able to do this at less cost to the state. In order to maximize profit, private prisons cut rehabilitation programs and medical

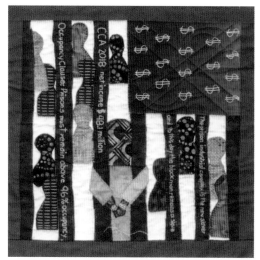

treatments for inmates. They instituted occupancy clauses in their contracts, holding the government legally responsible if the prisons are not full enough. A common requirement is 96 percent occupancy. This clause leads states to pressure their judicial and law enforcement agencies to enact laws and sentences that imprison individuals. Those who are targeted are often people of color who do not have the resources to fight against their injustice and oppression. This block uses the flag's stripes as prison bars to demonstrate that freedom from persecution is still not a liberty granted to all. The stars have been replaced with dollar signs as another indicator of how the American justice system profits off Black and Brown bodies."

## ROW 4, BLOCK 4: DEATH PENALTY BY SHEREE C.

"This block was inspired by *The Sun Does Shine*, the book and story of Anthony Ray Hinton. Hinton was wrongfully convicted and spent decades on death row even though there was definitive proof of his innocence. Hinton writes, 'They traded white hoods for black robes and called it the justice system.'

"The block's foundation is a mountain of mangled and discarded Brown and Black bodies. Atop that sits an electric chair with someone strapped in. On his prison jumper, and on some of the dead bodies, is embroidered the word 'innocent.' This illustrates the alarming statistic that one in ten people on death row are wrongfully convicted. The use of black and brown batiks highlights the disproportionate rate at which people of color are sentenced to death."

## ROW 5, BLOCK 1: UNARMED BY ANGELO M.

"When police officers kill an unarmed man, many people are quick to say, 'The officer had to make a split-second decision and it's a stressful job. Mistakes happen. Give them a break.' This rhetoric and support gives police a license to kill. Few people say, 'The victim was being yelled at by several officers. He was being given conflicting commands. He is an untrained civilian in a high-stress situation. He was likely to make a mistake.' This design shows an officer holding his suspect, a young Black man, at gunpoint. The officer, who is at a safe distance, asks for ID. The Black man pulls out his wallet and is shot. His ID and wallet tumble to the ground as the bullets hit his body. If only he had just complied with the officer's commands."

### ROW 5, BLOCK 2: MEMORIAL BY VICTORIA H.

"This quilt block was designed to sit in stark contrast with the introductory block depicting free African women and children. The somber colors of the piece represent the incomprehensible grief that Black people have faced since they were torn from their homelands. This memorial not only recognizes the murder of Black people at the hands of law enforcement, but it also stands in recognition of all the racial injustices that have led Black people in America to spiritual, emotional, and physical deaths. It is said that it is impossible for a Black man to be unarmed in America because his skin is the weapon he carries. The irrational fear of the predatory Black man or thug has had deadly consequences for Black boys.

"Since the death of Trayvon Martin in 2012, at least 66 other Black men and boys have been murdered by police under suspicious circumstances. The random items depicted here are some of the things that law enforcement mistook for weapons: cigarettes, CDs, wallets, pill bottles, and phones. Would these be viewed as innocuous if held by someone whose skin didn't label him a threat from birth?"

### ROW 5, BLOCK 3: THIN BLUE LINE BY JESSICA C.

"The oppressor always seeks to diminish a movement's voice by taking what a movement has created and saying, 'What about me?' In response to police violence, a movement was created to fight for the lives of Black people. This movement called itself Black Lives Matter. Those words caused outrage! New slogans such as All Lives Matter and, as in this block, Blue Lives Matter, were used to take away the voice of Black activists. Blue Lives Matter was the law enforcement community's counter to a movement that called for police accountability in the many murders of unarmed Black people. It was their 'Well, what about us?'

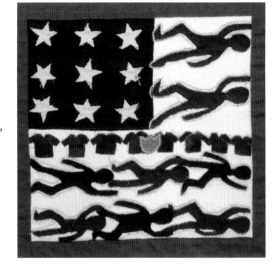

"This block replaces the black stripes of the Blue Lives Matter flag with the chalk-outlined corpses of Black men murdered by the police. The flag's 'thin blue line' is represented by officer uniforms that reflect the allegiance that police officers have to each other instead of to the justice system or to those they are charged to protect."

### ROW 5, BLOCK 4: BLACK LIVES MATTER BY JARON H.

"*When They Call You a Terrorist*, by Patrisse Khan-Cullors and Asha Bandele, is a fitting title for the memoir of the Black Lives Matter cofounder. It is an accurate description of the language that surrounds the Black Lives Matter movement. The fight for equality and recognition that Black Lives Matter represents has been spun by the media as an attack on fundamental American standards. The word *terrorism* is found throughout new legislative bills attempting to criminalize protest activities and activist political actions. My Black Lives Matter block symbolizes the strength of people coming together to take a stand against oppression."

# Memphis Art Teacher Blossoms into SJSA Workshop Facilitator: Jeannine La Bate

The opportunity to hand embroider unusual fabric-art pieces made by young people drew volunteer Jeannine La Bate into the Social Justice Sewing Academy. That first embroidery assignment soon blossomed into a central role with SJSA as a youth workshop facilitator across several states.

Jeannine is an art and fashion design instructor in the Memphis public high schools, and she has invested a lot of time and energy in educating students about the possibilities of using textile art for expression. So being part of SJSA is a natural extension of her mission.

Unfortunately, in the United States, most high schools have abandoned technical education curricula, such as sewing and home economics, and textile sewing classes are scarce at the college level. Jeannine was determined to bring them back to her classroom. And when she did, the result was amazing. From the very first day, when she introduced fabrics as the medium, her students were transformed. **Working with a needle and thread engaged the students in ways she had never seen, and that reinforced her idea that working with textiles is a way to connect to our history and make art with something that literally touches humans.**

Her grandmother sewed clothing, and Jeannine has vivid memories of watching her. She recognized that as she wore the clothing her grandmother constructed, she was carrying her grandmother's voice out into the world. Now, through SJSA, young people are continuing this tradition by sewing with textiles and amplifying their voice for the world to hear. While the messages are vastly different, textiles have a powerful way to communicate.

Jeannine La Bate has facilitated many workshops for SJSA, including this one with high school students in Memphis, Tennessee.

She also believes the adult volunteer component of SJSA is a powerful tool to engage embroiderers, sewists, quilters, and other artists with critical social issues. And being a part of this movement has even generated some surprising conversations with strangers. For example, when Jeannine went to a local coffee shop, she carried the youth block she was assigned with her to work on the hand embroidery stitches. The block contained fabric pieces and messages pertaining to LGBTQI+ lives. An older man approached her to ask what she was working on, and he was shocked to see pretty embroidery stitches being applied to something so unconventional. **The moment gave the two a rare opportunity to discuss the issues and social injustices faced by so many individuals.**

Most important for Jeannine, through art education in the high schools and the valuable workshops she facilitates for SJSA, she is instilling skills in young people that do not involve a smartphone or a computer screen. Her students are finding their own voice organically, and that is a lesson she hopes will last a lifetime.

**RIGHT:** The completion of *Inclusion* definitely took a village. First, Jeannine La Bate facilitated SJSA workshops in Memphis, Tennessee, where youth created the blocks. Next, quilter Tara Faughnan designed the color scheme and pattern for the overall quilt. Then Tara led a sewing-day gathering with experienced quilters and sewists at the Bay Quilts retail store in Richmond, California, where the blocks were pieced into the finished quilt. Finally, it was handed off to Nancy Williams for the final machine quilting.

**BELOW:** SJSA founder Sara Trail and other quilters participate in a special sewing day, led by Tara Faughnan, at the Bay Quilts store in Richmond, California, to complete the construction of the SJSA *Inclusion* community quilt.

**INCLUSION COMMUNITY QUILT**   BLOCKS MADE BY STUDENTS IN SJSA WORKSHOPS IN MEMPHIS, TENNESSEE
QUILT DESIGNED BY TARA FAUGHNAN AND SEWN BY VOLUNTEERS | MACHINE QUILTED BY NANCY WILLIAMS

# Quilter Sarah Bond Sees Hope

The Social Justice Sewing Academy mission is irresistible to Sarah Bond. Activism, art, and nurturing the creativity of young people are all things she is deeply passionate about, and for her, part of the attraction of SJSA is the fact that this organization is using textile art, more specifically quilts, to try to create a better future.

Sarah is an avid quiltmaker and quilting instructor, and she believes quilts are repositories of our daily lives. As such, they can teach us. That's part of her motivation to look back and learn from the quiltmakers who came before us. She has invested a considerable amount of time looking back at the quilts in her own family history, especially those made by her grandmothers, relatives, and close family friends. **She firmly believes that quilts are objects that carry a bit of each maker, and the stories of those makers will endure as long as the threads survive.** If we let them, these quilts can awaken us.

So an organization that embraces these same ideas and transfers them to young people is brilliant, in Sarah's view, and she eagerly wants to be a part of this effort. Dozens of individuals in each part of the construction process are touching these quilts—everyone from students to instructors, from the embroiderers to the final quilters. These quilts have a lot of hands on them, and Sarah takes comfort in the fact that all those hands are creating positive energy.

**In addition to all that energy coming from the assembly line of creative hands, these quilts also radiate hope, something she feels we all need more of right now.** Like most quiltmakers, Sarah mostly works alone in her studio, and the pandemic has increased our sense of isolation. For those who work alone, hope is hard to generate by yourself. These blocks have the power to deliver hope. Sarah feels the messages created on these textile blocks exert maturity, artistry, and awareness of today's issues, and prove that among these young makers, there is hope for a better future.

**TOP:** Talented quiltmakers such as Sarah Bond have donated countless hours to piece blocks together into finished quilts. Pre-Covid, this process might have been done in a twenty-first–century sewing circle, such as a quilt guild get-together.

**MIDDLE:** Quilter Sarah Bond created the beautifully pieced border surrounding this block for the *Declarations* community quilt.

**BOTTOM:** Black and white strips of fabric form the perfect border for this innovative block of artivist art.

**DECLARATIONS COMMUNITY QUILT**
MADE BY STUDENTS IN SJSA WORKSHOPS | PIECED BY SARAH BOND | MACHINE QUILTED BY NANCY WILLIAMS

**HEGEMONY COMMUNITY QUILT**
BLOCKS PIECED TOGETHER DURING THE COVID PANDEMIC
BY VOLUNTEERS AT CLOTH CAROUSEL IN VACAVILLE, CALIFORNIA
MACHINE QUILTED BY NANCY WILLIAMS | 2020

The word *hegemony* is defined as one group
or community holding authoritative power,
or dominance, over another.

Throughout history, women who agitated for the right to vote were seen as radicals. Susan B. Anthony was arrested. Ida B. Wells faced racist discrimination. Alice Paul was jailed and force-fed. Suffragists were maligned by society and took their activism to the streets to fight for their right to vote. Suffragists also used textiles to further their cause. Purple, white, and gold sashes reading, "Votes for Women"; banners with slogans like "Mr. President, how long must women wait for liberty?"; and the famous Ratification Banner became sewn icons of the suffrage movement.

The Social Justice Sewing Academy continues that tradition with *The Radicals*, inspired by the radical women of the early struggle for voting rights and the first female presidential nominee of a major party, Hillary Clinton. The struggle for suffrage is a complicated history, and voting rights remain a contentious topic to this day. The year 1920 marked the beginning of voting rights for White women, but systemic racism, including poll taxes, kept Black women from the polls. Indigenous women weren't granted citizenship until 1924, and Chinese women weren't able to become citizens until 1943, and therefore neither group could vote. While the 1965 Voting Rights Act opened the doors for more women to vote, it wasn't until ten years later that an expansion of the Voting Rights Act removed language tests that barred Hispanic Americans and other non-English–speaking Americans from voting. Today, barriers to voting remain for many people, including a lack of access to polling places and legislative pushes for voter ID laws. The young artists and artivists who made this quilt are working to raise awareness of the historical and contemporary fight for access to voting, and just like the suffragists who came before them, they too are seen as radicals.

### ROW 1: THE TRIAL OF SUSAN B. ANTHONY BY CARMEN A.

"Susan B. Anthony was not deterred from her activism due to her arrest and charge of illegal voting. She used the four months between her arrest and her trial to activate more people toward change. In June of 1873, the trial of Susan B. Anthony began. The courthouse was packed as Anthony entered, dressed in a petite dress and bonnet. In a two-day trial, the defense attempted to show that Anthony acted within her rights as she was a citizen of the United States. She was found guilty. Upon sentencing, Susan B. Anthony gave a speech.

*'Yes, your honor, I have many things to say; for in your ordered verdict of guilty, you have trampled underfoot every vital principle of our government. My natural rights, my civil rights, my political rights, my judicial rights, are all alike ignored. Robbed of the fundamental privilege of citizenship, I am degraded from the status of a citizen to that of a subject; and not only myself individually, but all of my sex, are, by your honor's verdict, doomed to political subjection under this, so-called, form of government.'*

"Anthony was found guilty and fined $100. She responded by telling the court that she would not pay the fine. True to her word, Susan B. Anthony never paid a penny of the fine that had been imposed upon her."

### ROW 1: HILLARY LOGO BY ERICA A.

"I chose to use Hillary Clinton's presidential campaign logo for this block. Presidential nominee Hillary Clinton's campaign was symbolic and memorable. Women around the world watched her engage in the political arena, recognizing that she was at a disadvantage because of her gender. 'I'm with her' and the bold **H** logo became unifying symbols for women, the community, and her campaign, along with the hashtag #imwithher."

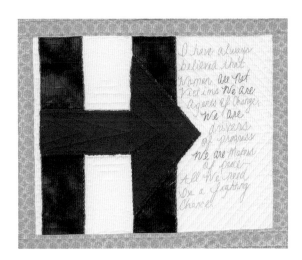

### ROW 1: ARRESTED FOR VOTING BY SAMANTHA B.

"On November 5, 1872, Susan B. Anthony bravely and calmly walked to the polls and demanded a ballot to vote.

When she was denied, she quoted the Fourteenth Amendment and threatened to bring charges and a suit against the registrars. Susan B. Anthony and eight other women cast their ballots. Later that day a complaint was lodged against Anthony for the act of illegal voting. She was arrested four days later. The warrant charged Anthony with voting in a federal election 'without having a lawful right to vote and in violation of section 19 of an act of Congress' enacted in 1870, commonly called The Enforcement Act, which carried a maximum penalty of $500 or three years' imprisonment."

**THE RADICALS COMMUNITY QUILT**
BLOCKS DESIGNED AND MADE BY HIGH SCHOOL STUDENTS
PIECED BY SARA TRAIL | MACHINE QUILTED BY NANCY WILLIAMS | 2020

### ROW 2: PRIMARIES PARTY BY ZIOMARA A.

"This block is a tribute to Hillary Clinton's Democratic National Convention (DNC) victory, where she was selected to be the 2016 Democratic nominee. On this day, Mrs. Clinton became the first woman to win the a major party's presidential nomination. The art shows her showered in balloons as supporters roar with excitement. I felt it was important to capture and highlight the excitement of a better nation that united the crowd."

### ROW 2: HILLARY CLINTON BY MARISSA B.

"Hillary Clinton has always acted as an advocate for women and children. She has been an inspiration to countless women and girls who didn't believe in their own strength and potential. Hillary Clinton's presidential campaign will forever act as inspiration for women in shattering the glass ceiling."

### ROW 3: ALICE PAUL BY VICTORIA C.

"Alice Paul started the Silent Sentinels movement in response to the difference she faced with the original suffragette leaders. She wanted to be more visible in her activism. She and a group of suffragettes picketed the parade the day before Woodrow Wilson's inauguration. This action led to the women being placed in jail, where they faced what is known as the Night of Terror. The women were beaten and terrorized by the jail guards. There are reports that they were lifted and slammed against metal tables and railings. In response to the beatings, her fellow suffragettes launched a hunger strike. In response to this political action, Alice Paul was removed and placed in the psychiatric unit. A feeding tube was forced down her throat and she was force-fed raw eggs."

### ROW 3: I VOTED TODAY BECAUSE OF HER BY JAMILAH F.

"Each year on Election Day in November, thousands of women visit Rochester, New York, to pay tribute to Susan B. Anthony by decorating her tombstone with 'I Voted Today' stickers. Susan B. Anthony was a pioneer in the suffrage movement who unfortunately did not live to see the Nineteenth Amendment passed. The placing of the stickers has become a pilgrimage for many women, who want to express the deep gratitude for their constitutional rights and honor this amazing woman who never stopped fighting or believing that one day women would have full citizenship."

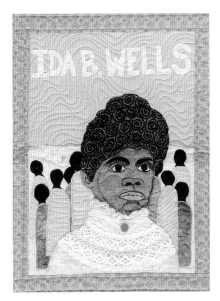

### ROW 3: IDA B. WELLS BY KATRINA D.

"Ida B. Wells led a life of advocacy. Ida was born into slavery and was freed with the declaration of the Emancipation Proclamation. Ida B. Wells was taught activism and the importance of education by her parents. She spent her life fighting against racism and sexism. She led anti-lynching campaigns and created a newspaper to circulate source material about lynch mobs and the injustices she was living and encountering. Ida was also the cofounder of the NAACP. She also founded the National Association of Colored Women. Ida B. Wells bridged the gap between the intersectionality of racism and sexism. She was a prominent Black feminist who recognized and spoke on behalf of the unique challenges that were facing Black women at the time. She was fearless and stood her ground in advocating for the rights of Black women in the suffrage movement."

### ROW 3: WHO WILL WEAR THE PANTS? BY VERONICA F.

"In response to the suffrage movement during the early 1920s, a series of political cartoons were published to devalue and debase women. The art in this block is a replication of a well-known poster during that era. The question 'What will men wear when women wear the pants?' highlights the fear anti-suffrage proponents spread in efforts to keep women from the polls. Those who opposed equal voting rights for women were not able to fathom the loss of control that they would have if women were equal in the political arena. Pants were a symbol of masculine strength while the dresses women were wearing were symbolic of weakness. How would the world change if women's voices were heard?"

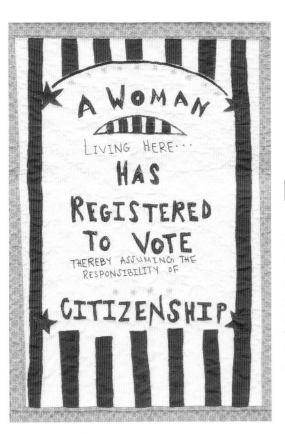

### ROW 4: A WOMAN VOTED BY SHERI W.

"This block is based on the 1919 design of a flyer or card that read, 'A Woman Living Here Has Registered to Vote.' The card was typically displayed in the window of a home. This became an act of solidarity, as voting was not always a popular action. Women during this time faced backlash from society and those who rallied to create the anti-suffrage movement. As with all social justice issues, there were disagreements among the community, friends, and family. The placing of the card in the window demonstrated that you and your household were on the right side of making history."

## ROW 4: PROTEST BY JOCELYN J.

"The suffragettes were outraged after the arrest of Alice Paul. They mobilized to create a movement to bring light to the treatment that the imprisoned suffragettes were enduring. The women stood their ground and demanded that Alice Paul be treated as a political prisoner since her crime was criticizing the government and fighting for her rights as a woman. Her crime was a struggle against ruling elites, and the suffragettes wanted her released."

## ROW 5: PRIMARIES MAP BY KYLE F.

"Imagine being on the edge of your seat waiting as the map turns colors and the votes roll in. Who will get the votes to secure the Democratic nomination for president? This block mimics the media screens we anxiously watch as the votes are revealed."

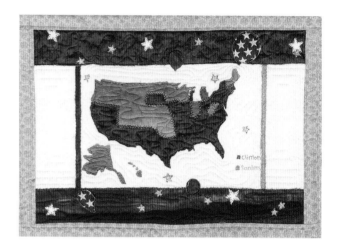

## ROW 5: THIS IS OUR MOVEMENT TOO BY JAZMYN F.

"When did women receive the right to vote? Most women know the answer to this question and will state that we are celebrating the 100th anniversary of women gaining that right with the passage of the Nineteenth Amendment. This date is only true if you do not consider Black women, women. All women did not gain the right to vote until the passage of the Civil Rights Act in 1965. It is not widely known that Black women were often excluded from women's rights activism. When Black women showed up to march, the organizers of the National American Woman Suffrage Association told the Black suffragettes that they were not welcome. They would need to form a group behind the White women so as not to be confused as part of the same movement.

"This block is an homage to the Black women, who fought for all women's right to vote and recognizes the unique plight of Black women who were faced with the issues that arose due to the intersection of race and gender. The feminist movement of the past was not inclusive of Black women. Many suffragettes were upset that the Black man won the right to vote before White women. There was also the sentiment that fighting for Black women would hinder the progress that White women could make."

# Scissors in a County Jail: *Art Behind Bars*

The idea of bringing scissors, needles, thread, fabric, and sewing machines into a county jail is radical, especially scissors and needles. But Emory Christian, former prosecutor turned educator, was able to persuade officials that the opportunity to work with the inmates and allow them to express their voice through textiles was a powerful educational opportunity.

Sixteen men between the ages of nineteen and their late 30s were chosen to participate in this program. Each of them was enrolled in the Five Keys Charter School, a special charter school that operates inside the San Francisco jails to help inmates obtain high school diplomas. But before the men chose their fabric and learned to sew, first they had some homework to do. They watched several documentaries and a movie about quiltmaking and had discussions about activist art. Finally, under Emory's instruction, they made a large community quilt for the Social Justice Sewing Academy titled *Art Behind Bars*.

**For Emory, the most remarkable thing about this program was how quickly these men "took" to sewing.** They mastered the machines and were quite adept at transferring their ideas to fabric. However, for security purposes, the scissors remained on a lanyard around Emory's neck, and she and another teacher did all the fabric cutting.

One of the things Emory believes this opportunity created is a rare chance for expression. Many of these men are stuck in their life path. They may or may not ever be convicted of a crime

because county jails hold individuals who are awaiting trial, those who cannot make bail, and those who are denied bail. So it is a difficult and stressful time for these men. **Creating art to voice their frustration with the system, the history of injustices they have faced, and the difficulties they face because of their race or socioeconomic status was therapeutic.** These classes allowed the men to sit with their emotions and find a way to share their innermost thoughts with everyone who views these quilts.

After thoughtfully choosing their messages, finding fabric to express their ideas, and finally threading needles and sewing, these men put their voices out there. Now it's up to the viewer to see them not just as inmates, but as whole individuals who have expressed themselves through this phenomenal community quilt.

**ART BEHIND BARS COMMUNITY QUILT**
MADE DURING AN SJSA WORKSHOP
IN A SAN FRANCISCO COUNTY JAIL
SIXTEEN INMATES PARTICIPATED
MACHINE QUILTED BY NANCY WILLIAMS

***LAKOTA YOUTH SPEAK* COMMUNITY QUILT**
MADE IN 2018 DURING YOUTH WORKSHOPS ON CHEYENNE RIVER RESERVATION, SOUTH DAKOTA | MACHINE QUILTED BY NANCY WILLIAMS

Youth from Cheyenne River Reservation in South Dakota participate in an SJSA workshop as part of a series of efforts aimed at helping these students attain restorative justice and amplify Indigenous voices.

**SUSTAINABILITY COMMUNITY QUILT**
BLOCKS DESIGNED BY YOUNG PEOPLE IN SJSA WORKSHOPS
EMBROIDERED BY SJSA VOLUNTEERS
PIECED AND CONSTRUCTED BY MEMBERS OF EAST BAY HERITAGE QUILTERS
WITH DIRECTION FROM MARTHA WOLFE
MACHINE QUILTED BY NANCY WILLIAMS

This quilt was pieced with an improvisational style using denim clothing found in thrift stores.

# How the *Harmony* Community Quilt Caused Disharmony in the Quilt Community

> "Backlash over the block's perceived political undertones led to charges of intolerance. Then, new versions of the design set off a second round of angry posts and a debate over whether the changes made their work ineligible for a highly coveted label they can receive for assembling 12 challenge blocks into a quilt."
> ■ Peggy McGlone, *Washington Post* (January 20, 2020)

When a young student named Leland created a pictorial textile block during a Social Justice Sewing Academy workshop in Baltimore, he created the inspiration for a pivotal SJSA outreach program, as well as an opportunity for discourse. Leland's block featured the word *inequality* and a pencil erasing the letters "*in*."

**The discourse started in 2019, when the SJSA was invited to exhibit a selection of artivist quilts at the National Quilt Museum in Paducah, Kentucky.** As part of that exhibition, the nonprofit group offered the 100,000-plus members of the museum the opportunity to participate in a Block of the Month program. This program is sponsored by the National Quilt Museum, and the goal is to challenge participants to learn and master new stitching and quilt piecing techniques, while constructing quilt block patterns that coincide with an exhibition at the museum. Typically, the quilters would construct one block each month, with the goal of ultimately piecing the blocks together into one large quilt.

One of the monthly patterns, introduced by SJSA, was inspired by Leland's block in the *Harmony* community quilt. Pattern designer Melinda Newton, along with SJSA founder Sara Trail, changed the word to *injustice* and kept the image of the pencil erasing the letters "*in*."

What happened next is something SJSA will never forget. Immediately after the pattern was introduced, several hundred participants took to the museum's Facebook page to voice opposition. Comments pro and con were flying back and forth. Those in opposition to the Injustice block cited it as political and expressed their opinion that the National Quilt Museum program should be apolitical. Others supported the block and urged unity.

National Quilt Museum CEO Frank Bennett quickly issued statements supporting the block and requested all participants to be inclusive. SJSA also participated in the dialogue and encouraged everyone to consider the Injustice block pattern as a positive message. National media also took note of the controversy, and the *Washington Post* published an article on January 20, 2020, under the headline, "Now, Even Quilters Are Angry: How a Social-Justice Design Started a Feud."

The good news is, for SJSA, the Block of the Month program has gone on to have new life beyond the National Quilt Museum. **Now, supporters of the organization are stepping up to make their own blocks, and many participants are finishing the series and showing off their finished SJSA quilts.** Engaging quilters and sewists in this way is yet another important outreach program for SJSA to continue the dialogue and force the conversation.

**HARMONY COMMUNITY QUILT**
CREATED BY STUDENTS IN BALTIMORE, MARYLAND
BLOCK PATTERN DESIGNED BY MELINDA NEWTON
MACHINE QUILTED BY NANCY WILLIAMS

The block with the word **inequality** (*top row, far right*) was created by a student named Leland. His block became the inspiration for a block pattern designed by Melinda Newton. For this pattern, Melinda and SJSA changed the word to *injustice*. This one little block, and the selection of just one word, caused an uproar among some quilters in early 2020.

**SAY THEIR NAMES** MADE USING A REVERSE APPLIQUÉ METHOD SARA WAS INSPIRED TO MAKE BY WELL-KNOWN ARTIVIST AND QUILTER CHAWNE KIMBER | BY SARA TRAIL | 2017

**TWITTER TANTRUMS**   55″ × 60″
COTTON, BATIKS, DONATED FABRIC APPLIQUÉ | HAND EMBROIDERY
BY CARINA CABRIALES | MACHINE QUILTED BY NANCY WILLIAMS, 2017

## In the Words of Carina Cabriales

"A '*Twitter tantrum*,' as defined by Urban Dictionary, '*occurs when a Twitter user is at odds with one or more of his/her fellow Twitterers. This is typically characterized by a confrontational exchange of 'tweets' during which threats are made to unfollow (block), etc. This is not atypical behavior considering the often self-absorbed and self-serving personality traits of the participants and their insatiable need for attention and validation.*' These words also accurately describe the 45th president. **Through his tweets he has appealed to white supremacist rhetoric, and validated and endorsed racist, misogynistic, hateful, and violent behavior and mindsets.** He has made it okay to be dishonest, he has made it okay to be morally bankrupt, he has made it okay to objectify women. Unfortunately, and with regularity, more of these hurtful, divisive, hateful words come from our 45th president every day. *This is not normal!*"

**BLACK QUEENS**   43″ × 46″ | COTTON | RAW-EDGE APPLIQUÉ, HAND EMBROIDERY
BY CRYSTAL WARD | MACHINE QUILTED BY NANCY WILLIAMS | 2018

## In the Words of Crystal Ward

"The conversation about inequity, violence, and marginalization often omits the group of people most disenfranchised in the world—Black women. Yet despite the literal disrespect and omission from the conversation, #blackgirlmagic is at the forefront and stronger than ever. **Black women are trend setters, nurturers, healers, activists, and often the brilliance behind political, religious, and social movements.** Black women make up the fastest-growing group of entrepreneurs in America, are being elected into political office, and now more than ever are unapologetically letting their voice, experience, and stories be heard. This mini quilt titled *Black Queens* shows a stunning Black woman with a crown placed atop her head to signify both her importance and her regality. This depiction of a Black Queen stands in contrast to the famous Malcolm X quote as a juxtaposition that shows the strength and resilience we all have. It is time for Black women to get their due respect, recognition, and equality."

**EXIT WOUND**
55″ × 60″ | COTTON
RAW-EDGE APPLIQUÉ, HAND EMBROIDERY
BY AUDREY BERNIER
MACHINE QUILTED BY NANCY WILLIAMS
2018

## In the Words of Audrey Bernier

"I created this quilt starting with the idea of oranges. Did you know that the exit wounds from an AR-15 are the size of an orange? Regardless of the shooter's aim, if he hits anything, he's going to do severe damage—more often than not, fatal damage. I titled my quilt *Exit Wound* as a reminder that gun control in all communities is a social justice issue that deserves action and conversation. The murders at Marjory Stoneman Douglas High School, Parkland, Florida, really shook America to its core and sparked a national conversation, led by young people, around gun control. They also highlighted the difference in response of outrage when mass shootings occur in privileged areas versus underresourced areas.

Audrey Bernier designing her quilt *Exit Wound*

"Being born and raised in Baltimore, I am no stranger to gun violence—many peers of mine have been killed by a bullet, and this epidemic has been persistent in Baltimore for years. **What troubles me is that the deaths of my friends go unnoticed on the national stage, while the deaths of more privileged children create a national movement.** The issues of social justice and gun violence are important right now because young people everywhere are tired of sitting back and waiting for adults to change policies. I believe that AR-15–style weapons and high-capacity gun clips should be banned for use by civilians in the United States, once and for all. We need to understand that we can use our voices as young people and empower our communities so that we prevent more people from dying."

## In the Words of Audrey Bernier

"The racial profiling of those of Latin descent has grown with significant intensity. SB1070, a legislative bill that originated out of Arizona, gave law enforcement the power to stop anyone whose appearance indicated they might be from a different country. They were then allowed to ask for proof of citizenship, and any individual over eighteen who could not provide this was charged with a misdemeanor. This systemic targeting had serious repercussions, leading individuals who had committed no other crime to be deported and those here legally to be in jeopardy of losing their immigration status over a failure to carry a document. **Eventually the Supreme Court ruled that the racial profiling aspect of this bill was unconstitutional but upheld the right for law enforcement to demand proof of citizenship and detain an individual if it was not provided.**

"Like all systems of oppression, the detainment of immigrants would not be hindered and has grown into a border patrol policy that allows for the stopping of any desired person within 100 miles of any border and permission to ask for proof of citizenship. The ACLU estimates two-thirds of all people live within this region and are subject to this allowed abuse of our Fourth-Amendment constitutional right against unreasonable search and seizure.

"In recent years America has begun to specifically target and detain immigrants of Latinx origin through Immigration and Customs Enforcement (ICE) raids. With the aid of many local law enforcement agencies, the ICE has begun to attack work sites, school drop-offs, and designated safe havens, dragging suspected immigrants away to camps that are overcrowded and lack basic care and necessities. Families are impacted when children are separated from their families, either by being in detention or by being greeted by an empty home upon arriving from school. Young children are kept caged in these camps until they are given immigration hearings, which they must face without guardianship or legal aid.

"One of the largest private prison companies, CCA, acquired the contracts to maintain and continue to build immigration camps. This is the corporation that has occupancy clauses for its prisons whereby the government is required to pay substantial fines if there are not enough people locked up. Each individual who is detained is a dollar sign for legislators and for this corporation. The prolonged detention of immigrants, like all acts of oppression, has created a cycle of wealth and influence for those involved in its creation and implementation."

*AMERICAN SCREAM*   40˝ × 60˝ | COTTON | RAW-EDGE APPLIQUÉ
BY AUDREY BERNIER | MACHINE QUILTED BY NANCY WILLIAMS | 2019

**KALIEF BROWDER: JUSTICE DENIED** 44″ × 50″
COTTON | APPLIQUÉ, HAND EMBROIDERY | BY KAILAH FOREMAN
MACHINE QUILTED BY NANCY WILLIAMS | 2018

This quilt was awarded second place in the youth category at the 2019 Modern Quilt Guild QuiltCon.

## In the Words of Kailah Foreman

"I created this quilt to remind people that the prison system is a continuation of slavery. Did you know there are more African Americans in the criminal justice system today than the number enslaved in 1850?

**When the Thirteenth Amendment was passed, most people believed that slavery was over.** However, there is a small clause in there that hides an exception; the amendment actually reads that slavery shall no longer exist in the United States 'except as punishment for crime whereof the party shall have been duly convicted.' America has boldly exploited that clause to great profit since then. A young teenager in New York City named Kalief Browder was locked up for nearly three years over a crime he didn't commit. This quilt is to remind America that we haven't forgotten about Kalief Browder, and there are likely thousands of other Browders still trapped in other systems as well."

## Exquisite Art from a Young Artist: Bryan Robinson

■ Bryan Robinson has lived in the same neighborhood his whole life. His grandmother lives next door, and aunts, uncles, and cousins live close by. So it is especially frustrating for Bryan when he walks his dog along the streets he knows so well and looks up to notice that his newly transplanted White neighbors often eye him warily.

While being stuck at home during the Covid pandemic, sometimes Bryan gets in his car to just drive around. But this seemingly simple way of passing the time comes with considerable risk. As a young Black man, Bryan is repeatedly stopped by law enforcement. When he was on his way to the hospital to visit his elderly grandfather, he was stopped. When there was an active search for a criminal in the area, Bryan was stopped. And on some days, for seemingly no reason at all, he is stopped. This is the reality that he lives with. And each and every time, he prays that he won't come face to face with an anxious or overzealous police officer, or worse, find a gun pointing at his body.

**For Bryan, having guns pointed at you is a very real threat.** At one point, in the midst of a crime scene that brought multiple police cars, vans, and snipers planted on rooftops to Bryan's neighborhood, he walked outside to see what was going on. Before he knew it, there were more than a dozen guns pointed right at him.

Bryan's ten-year-old brother once asked him, "Why do they kill us?" He had no answer, and he tries not to let these things upset him. These incidents, and all the unanswered questions, are just facts of life that he cannot change. **Bryan chooses to see the brighter side of life and tries to be joyful.** His smile is darling, and one cannot help but feel drawn in by his gregarious personality and chatty nature, even though there was a point in his life as a young child when he stopped talking altogether. When he was just five years old, his father "was taken from" the family and sent to prison. Those were tough years for Bryan, his mom, and their family. But his father was eventually released, and today, Bryan and his father have a close relationship.

The frustrations, the pain, and the racial stereotyping that interrupt Bryan's life are emotions that he kept buried until he met Sara Trail in 2016 and joined her workshop at the University of California, Berkeley. Sara's six-week social justice workshop for high school students, under the Upward Bound program, changed Bryan's life—even though he almost walked out the first day. Originally, Bryan assumed a workshop on social justice would be a history class. But once he entered the room, he found a dozen sewing machines and piles of fabric. Bryan was confused and certain he was in the wrong class. Fortunately, he stuck it out, and among those piles of fabric, scissors, glue, and sewing machines, Bryan discovered his voice.

For the first time, he began to think differently about his own situation and how his life had been impacted. **Being able to transform his frustrations toward systemic racism into art gave Bryan an entirely new perspective.** His first quilt dealt with gun violence. He was so enthralled with it that he went on to make a second quilt. This one was infinitely more personal. The quilt is titled *Blood, White & Blue* (at right), and it is an incredibly intense artistic expression that immediately commands the viewer's attention. It is a work that could easily have been made by an artist with decades of experience making political art with textiles, yet it was made by a teenager expressing his own daily struggles. Running along the stripes of the American flag are haunting images of dark bodies hanging from nooses. Amid these figures is Bryan, dressed in a graduation cap and gown, giving hope to the overall piece.

These quilts have been exhibited all over the United States, featured in magazines, and widely shared on social media, and they are helping thousands of people hear Bryan's voice. When his mother came to one exhibition, her son's art brought tears to her eyes. She saw his talent first-hand and realized her son had grown up to be a bright young man who is finding a way to express himself and share his feelings with the world.

## In the Words of Bryan Robinson

"The American flag has historically stood as a symbol of freedom and patriotism for our nation. It is the relic we are asked to pledge allegiance to and is flown at half-staff to communicate mourning, distress, or respect. In making this quilt I wanted to highlight and acknowledge the hidden and often dismissed history of our American flag—one where the stars and stripes that connote freedom cover the blood of my ancestors, people of color, and Indigenous people who gravely suffered, gave their life, or were exploited while building this nation. **In the present day, our country still suffers from the residue of slavery and unaddressed centering of White normative standards and systems of power and privilege.**

"I represented the dichotomous history of our flag by maintaining the structure of the flag while making key design choices that highlight injustice—the red stripes appear as dripping blood to recognize the blood on our hands as a nation in systematically and violently oppressing people of color, the white stripes show hanging bodies to represent a stark contrast to the perceived 'purity' of the color, and the stars represent outlines of killers and their victims. You'll notice one body that is hanging has a graduation cap; that is me. I chose to put myself in the quilt to acknowledge that no matter how much I push against the system of oppression to defy the low expectations and stereotypical narratives of Black men and boys, I am always going to be left unprotected and at risk of being seen as a dangerous threat, and that the reality of this is painful, unfair, and unjust."

**BLOOD, WHITE & BLUE**   60″ × 80″
COTTON | RAW-EDGE APPLIQUÉ, HAND EMBROIDERY
BY BRYAN ROBINSON | MACHINE QUILTED BY NANCY WILLIAMS

# Juan Tapia's Voice and the Unexpected Art of Quilting

■ In his early twenties, Juan Tapia found his voice in the unexpected medium of quilting. The experience changed him profoundly.

**Growing up in a dense, urban area of Oakland, California, Juan and his family were renters who were continually forced to move as the community around them gentrified.** One home after another was sold out from under them. Many were torn down are replaced with new construction targeting wealthy owners.

The constant disruption of moving made for a chaotic home life, and when Juan chose to attend a Social Justice Sewing Academy workshop, at first, he had no idea how the experience would generate so much opportunity. Juan and Bryan Robinson were both students at the same 2016 workshop, at the University of California, Berkeley. The six-week program was led by Sara Trail, under the Upward Bound program. As Sara challenged the students to focus on the life issues that were most critical to them, Juan gravitated toward the injustices of gentrification.

***GENTRIFY THIS*** MADE AND MACHINE QUILTED BY JUAN TAPIA | 2016

Once the quilt was finished, Juan began joining Sara in multiple public speaking opportunities (before Covid), where he has shared his story. **He has no doubts that quilting, and the subsequent public speaking, helped him find his voice and to see the world in a new way.** He is currently working at a nonprofit doing graphic design and community activism.

As Juan's voice is being amplified he is turning the tables, and the student has become the teacher. Juan is determined to empower young people in his community with the same opportunity to express themselves. By doing so, he embodies the whole intent of SJSA by bringing textile arts to young people as a way to raise their voice and make it heard.

# SJSA Expands Yosief Teckle's Definition of Art

■ Art, especially drawing, has always been a favorite hobby of Yosief Teckle's. But up until he attended a Social Justice Sewing Academy workshop, he assumed art was just that—a hobby. **He now sees the possibilities that art can open up as a means to express opinions, even outrage.** Furthermore, based on his experiences in this "very cool" workshop, Yosief has even considered a possible career as a graphic designer.

Yosief was born in Eritrea, in East Africa, and he moved to Oakland, California, with his mother and brother in 2014. In high school, he was chosen to participate in an arts elective program at the public high school, and that led to his decision to participate in the 2016 workshop at the University of California, Berkeley, which was led by Sara Trail, under the Upward Bound program. Unlike many students in that program, Yosief actually had some experience sewing clothing as a young boy. But he says he still had a lot to learn about sewing appliqué pieces for a complex art quilt using today's modern sewing machines.

One side benefit of participating in this workshop was the opportunity to be surrounded by other young people of color who had similar backgrounds and shared an interest in art. During those sessions, it was an eye-opening experience to see how creative these students were and how openly they expressed their opinions. **Yosief's quilt has toured to exhibitions around the United States, and he is thrilled to know that so many people have had an opportunity to see his quilt.**

And now that a few years have passed, Yosief admits he'd like to make another art quilt. Being creative, whether he is drawing or making a quilt, is something he turns to again and again to relieve the stress of a busy college life. Possibly, one day in the future, he will create another memorable work of textile art and have another chance to express his point of view and share it with the world.

PROTECT AND SERVE? MADE DURING AN SJSA WORKSHOP AND MACHINE QUILTED BY YOSIEF TECKLE | 2016

## In the Words of Yosief Teckle

"Despite repeating the phrase, 'I can't breathe' eleven times on July 17, 2014, 43-year-old Eric Garner died from a choke hold in the hands of the very people we look to for protection—the police. **As a child, I was always taught to never run from and always respect the police, but with countless lives being lost at the hands of the police I wonder if the respect is mutual.** This sewing opportunity allowed me to express my creativity in a way that encompassed current social issues, and I enjoyed it much more than expected."

**PICTURED FROM LEFT:** Juan Tapia, Cedric Tanner, Sara Trail, Bryan Robinson, Jocelyn Gama Garcia, Yosief Teckle, and Amin Robinson

# CONCLUSION—STEP UP AND LEARN MORE

**The words and images on these pages capture the beginning of a movement.**
The movement did not begin, or end, with George Floyd's death. Rather, the Social Justice Sewing Academy is a critical part of the dialogue that has been ongoing for years and must continue in the future. SJSA has chosen the route of textile art and quilts to send its message out into the world and to engage both makers and viewers.

Through SJSA, many volunteers are transformed into artivists. They are stepping up and making their own voice heard by creating art with a message and art that honors another human being. We encourage everyone to be a part of this—make a quilt for a family that has lost a loved one, or make a block honoring a victim. Be active. Step up. Force the conversation.

If you are not a maker, you can also support SJSA through donations. Or you can volunteer. SJSA is a grassroots, volunteer organization. We need volunteers in a variety of roles, including workshop hosting, coordinating exhibitions, administrative support, web / social media support, and many other opportunities.

Please visit the SJSA website (page 175). Educators, workshop facilitators, and other groups or individuals will find helpful guides and curriculum. The site is continually updated with resources, including an anti-racist guide, workshop instructions, and information on how to have a conversation and elevate the voices of the unheard. There are also links to organizations that support the families of victims, as well as general educational materials and social justice information.

The Social Justice Sewing Academy Remembrance Project is a twenty-first–century sewing circle.

# INDEX

Key to additional photo locations: **FC** = front cover • **FE** = front endpapers • **BC** = back cover • **BE** = back endpapers

## ADDITIONAL PHOTOGRAPHY CREDITS

# ABOUT THE AUTHORS

## SARA TRAIL

Sara Trail learned to sew at the young age of four, and she is now a successful author, sewing teacher, and pattern and fabric designer. At age thirteen, she wrote a nationally published book, *Sew with Sara* (from C&T Publishing), that teaches teens and tweens how to sew cute clothes and accessories for fun and profit. At fifteen, she starred in a nationally published DVD series, *Cool Stuff to Sew with Sara* (from C&T Publishing).

She then designed two fabric collections, Folkheart and Biology 101, and a pattern collection with Simplicity, Designed with Love by Sara. Her pattern collection features prom dresses, backpack patterns, hoodies, and jackets, as well as aprons and tote bags.

**While attending UC Berkeley, Sara created a quilt in memory of Trayvon Martin, and her love for sewing and passion for social justice intertwined.** After graduating from the Harvard University Graduate School of Education, she founded the Social Justice Sewing Academy (SJSA) to empower individuals to use textile art as a framework for activism.

## TERESA DURYEA WONG

Teresa Duryea Wong is a lifelong writer and communicator. She began her career as a television journalist and later spent several years as the publisher of a fine art magazine. For two decades, she worked for large corporations and eventually became an executive. When her two children left for college, Teresa left the corporate world and decided to return to college as well, earning a master of liberal studies degree from Rice University. In July 2020, she became a member of the International Advisory Board of the International Quilt Museum.

Teresa is author of four nonfiction art history books covering Japanese quilts and textiles, as well as American quilt history and cotton farming. **She currently works as a researcher, writer, and lecturer, and is an avid quiltmaker.** Learn more about Teresa and her other books at teresaduryeawong.com.

## ALSO BY SARA TRAIL
*Available as an eBook*

## VISIT THE SOCIAL JUSTICE SEWING ACADEMY ONLINE AND FOLLOW ON SOCIAL MEDIA!

**Website**
sjsacademy.org

**Facebook**
/socialjusticesewingacademy

**Instagram**
@sjsacademy
@sjsa_remembranceproject

**Twitter**
@sjsacademy

Hundreds of volunteers created artistic textile blocks honoring victims of violent crimes who lived in their communities. The blocks were joined into a quilted banner, which was stitched, finished, and quilted by yet another volunteer.

Volunteers hold up SJSA Remembrance Project banners in front of an urban mural in Houston's Heights neighborhood.